Marvin R. Vincent

A History of the textual Criticism of the New Testament

Marvin R. Vincent

A History of the textual Criticism of the New Testament

ISBN/EAN: 9783743335592

Manufactured in Europe, USA, Canada, Australia, Japa

Cover: Foto ©Lupo / pixelio.de

Manufactured and distributed by brebook publishing software
(www.brebook.com)

Marvin R. Vincent

A History of the textual Criticism of the New Testament

New Testament Handbooks

EDITED BY

SHAILER MATHEWS

A HISTORY OF

THE TEXTUAL CRITICISM OF THE NEW TESTAMENT

New Testament Handbooks

EDITED BY SHAILER MATHEWS
THE UNIVERSITY OF CHICAGO

A series of volumes presenting briefly and intelligibly the results of the scientific study of the New Testament. Each volume covers its own field, and is intended for the general reader as well as the special student.

Arrangements have been made for the following volumes:—

THE HISTORY OF THE TEXTUAL CRITICISM OF THE NEW TESTAMENT. Professor MARVIN R. VINCENT, Union Theological Seminary. [*Ready.*

THE HISTORY OF THE HIGHER CRITICISM OF THE NEW TESTAMENT. Professor HENRY S. NASH, Cambridge Divinity School.

INTRODUCTION TO THE BOOKS OF THE NEW TESTAMENT. Professor B. WISNER BACON, Yale Divinity School.

THE HISTORICAL GEOGRAPHY OF THE NEW TESTAMENT. Professor J. R. S. STERRETT, Amherst College.

THE HISTORY OF NEW TESTAMENT TIMES IN PALESTINE. Professor SHAILER MATHEWS, The University of Chicago. [*Ready.*

THE LIFE OF PAUL. President RUSH RHEES, The University of Rochester.

THE HISTORY OF THE APOSTOLIC AGE. Dr. C. W. VOTAW, The University of Chicago.

THE TEACHING OF JESUS. Professor GEORGE B. STEVENS, Yale Divinity School.

THE BIBLICAL THEOLOGY OF THE NEW TESTAMENT. Professor E. P. GOULD. [*In Preparation.*

THE TEACHING OF JESUS AND MODERN SOCIAL PROBLEMS. Professor FRANCIS G. PEABODY, Harvard Divinity School.

THE HISTORY OF CHRISTIAN LITERATURE UNTIL EUSEBIUS. Professor J. W. PLATNER, Harvard Divinity School.

PREFACE

THIS volume is simply what its title imports, — a History of the Textual Criticism of the New Testament, in which the attempt is made to exhibit its development in a form available for New Testament students who have not given special attention to the subject, and to direct such to the sources for more detailed study, if they are so inclined. It is gathered from sources which are indicated under the several topics and which are well known to textual scholars. The great interest awakened during the last few years by the special discussions of the Codex Bezæ has led me to assign considerable space to these, and the section on this subject has been prepared for this volume by my valued friend and colleague and former pupil, the Rev. James Everett Frame of Union Theological Seminary.

MARVIN R. VINCENT.

v

PART I

NATURE AND SOURCES OF THE TEXTUAL CRITICISM OF THE NEW TESTAMENT

CHAPTER I

CHAPTER II

CHAPTER III

A
HISTORY OF THE TEXTUAL CRITICISM OF THE NEW TESTAMENT

———••◦>◦◦<◦••———

PART I

NATURE AND SOURCES OF THE TEXTUAL CRITICISM OF THE NEW TESTAMENT

———••◦•———

CHAPTER I

THE NEED AND OFFICE OF TEXTUAL CRITICISM

TEXTUAL CRITICISM is that process by which it is sought to determine the original text of a document or of a collection of documents, and to exhibit it, freed from all the errors, corruptions, and variations which it may have accumulated in the course of its transmission by successive copyings. *Introductory definitions.*

A text is the body of words employed by an author in the composition of a document; as by Thucydides, in his *History of the Peloponnesian War;* by Dante in the *Divina Commedia;* or by Paul in the Epistle to the Romans.

The word "text" is also applied to the body of words which constitutes an edition of an original document. Thus we speak of Lachmann's text of Lucretius, or of Witte's text of the *Divina Commedia,* or of Westcott and Hort's text of Romans and Galatians.

These editions may approximate more or less to the texts of the original documents; but unless they exactly reproduce those texts, they are not the texts of Lucretius, of Dante, or of Paul. There can be but one text of a document, and that is the body of words written by the author himself. The text of a document, accurately speaking, is that which is contained in its autograph.

Original text of a document.

This is not to say that the autograph is without error. When we speak of the original text of a document, we mean only that it is what the author himself wrote, including whatever mistakes the author may have made. Every autograph is likely to contain such mistakes. The most careful writer for the press, on reading his work in print, often discovers omissions of words, incomplete sentences, unconscious substitutions of other words for those which he had intended to write, careless constructions which make his meaning ambiguous, or unintentional insertions of words which materially modify the sense which he meant to convey. These things are the results of lapses of attention or memory, or of temporary diversions of thought. In the preparation of matter for the press, such errors are mostly corrected by careful proof-reading; but before the invention of printing, when hand-copying was the only means of publication, they were much more likely to be perpetuated.

The original document not necessarily without errors.

It is entirely possible that a careful transcription of a document by an intelligent and accurate scribe, a transcription in which the errors of the original were corrected, should have been really a better piece of work than the autograph itself, and, on the whole, more satisfactory to the author: only the revised copy was not the original text.

The New Testament is no exception to this rule. If the autographs of the Pauline Epistles, for instance, should be recovered, they would no doubt be found to contain errors such as have been described. "If we consider that the authors themselves or their amanuenses in dictation may have made mistakes, and that the former, in revision, may have introduced improvements and additions, — the question arises whether the text ever existed in complete purity at all, and in what sense" (Reuss).[1]

The problem for the textual critic of the New Testament grows out of the fact that the New Testament autographs have disappeared, and with them all copies earlier than the middle of the fourth century. The contents of the original manuscripts can, therefore, be only approximately determined, through a comparison of later copies, all of which are more or less

Problem for the textual critic.

---

[1] Nothing can be more puerile or more desperate than the effort to vindicate the divine inspiration of Scripture by the assertion of the verbal inerrancy of the autographs, and to erect that assertion into a test of orthodoxy. For : —

1. There is no possible means of verifying the assertion, since the autographs have utterly disappeared.

2. It assumes a mechanical dictation of the *ipsissima verba* to the writers, which is contradicted by the whole character and structure of the Bible.

3. It is of no practical value, since it furnishes no means of deciding between various readings or discrepant statements.

4. It is founded upon a pure assumption as to the character of inspiration — namely, that inspiration involves verbal inerrancy, which is the very thing to be proved, and which could be proved only by producing inerrant autographs.

5. If a written, inspired revelation is necessary for mankind, and if such a revelation, in order to be inspired, must be verbally inerrant, the necessity has not been met. There is no verbally inerrant, and therefore no inspired, revelation in writing. The autographs have vanished, and no divine guidance or interposition has prevented mistakes in transcription or in printing. The text of Scripture, in the best form in which critical scholarship can exhibit it, presents numerous errors and discrepancies.

faulty, and which exhibit numerous differences. These copies have been made from other copies, and these in turn from others. The critic has no evidence that any copy in his possession has been made directly from the original; or, if there should be such a copy, which one it is. Pages of the two oldest copies known to us have evidently been written by the same scribe, yet their differences show that both were not copied from the same original. From the fact that a manu-

An early date does not prove a purer text.

script is of very early date, it cannot be assumed that its text is correspondingly purer, that is, more nearly approaching the autograph. It must first be settled how many copies there are between it and the autograph, and whether it followed an earlier or a later copy, and whether the copy which it followed correctly represented the autograph or not. A fourth-century manuscript, for instance, may have been copied from one only a few years earlier than itself; while an eleventh-century manuscript may have been copied from one of the third century, and that in turn from the autograph; so that the later manuscript may exhibit a purer text than the earlier. Let it be borne in mind that the critic is searching, not for the oldest manuscript, but for the oldest text.

In the multiplication of written copies errors were inevitable. Every new copy was a new source of error, since a copyist was likely not only to transcribe the errors of his exemplar, but also to make additional mistakes of his own. These errors might be conscious or unconscious, intentional or unintentional. A scribe,

Causes of copyists' errors.

for example, might confuse two capital letters of similar appearance, as Є, C (Ϲ); O, Θ. Or the similarity of two letters might cause him to overlook the one and pass directly to the other, as ΠΡΟΕΛΘΩΝ for ΠΡΟϹ–ΕΛΘΩΝ. Or letters might be transposed, as C̄ΡΙΑΝ (σωτηριαν) for C̄ΡΑῙΝ (σωτηρα Ιησουν). Again, if two consecutive lines in the exemplar ended with the same word or syllable, the copyist's eye might catch the second line instead of the first, and he would omit the intermediate words. In the early days of the church many copies were made hurriedly, and mistakes were sure to arise from hasty transcription. So long as the scribe confined himself to the purely mechanical work of copying, the errors would be chiefly those of sight, hearing, or memory ; when he began to think for himself, more mischief was done. The working of his own mind on the subject might move him to introduce a word which did not appear in his exemplar. He might find in the margin of his exemplar some oral tradition, like the story of the angel who troubled the pool of Bethzatha; or some liturgical fragment, like the doxology of the Lord's Prayer; or some explanatory comment, and incorporate these into the text. There were many who would have the books of approved authors in a fuller rather than in a shorter form, through fear of losing something of what the author had said. Bengel remarks, "Many learned men are not easily persuaded to regard anything as superfluous." Porson [1] says that, so far from its being an affected or absurd idea that a marginal note can ever creep into the text, it has actually happened in millions of places. Again, a scribe might alter a text in one Gospel in order to make it conform to a parallel passage in another; or he might change an unclassical word or expression for a more classical one. Such things would be fruitful sources of variation.[2]

Careless-ness.

Interpolation.

Deliberate alteration.

[1] Letters to Travis.

[2] The causes of variation will be found treated in detail in Scrivener's *Introduction to the Criticism of the New Testament*, 4th ed., I, 7-19. Also in Schaff's *Companion to the Greek Testament*, 183, and the excellent little treatise of C. E. Hammond, *Textual Criticism Applied to the New Testament.*

It will be seen, therefore, that the task of the textual critic is no easy one. As early as 1707, Dr. Mill estimated the number of variations in the New Testament text at 30,000; but this estimate was based on a comparatively few manuscripts. To-day, the number of Greek manuscripts discovered and catalogued, and containing the whole or portions of the New Testament, is estimated at 3829, and the number of actual variations in existing documents is reckoned roughly from 150,000 to 200,000.[1]

Number of actual variations.

This, however, does not mean that there is that number of places in the New Testament where various readings occur. It merely represents the sum total of various readings, each variation being counted as many times as it appears in different documents. For instance, taking some given standard and comparing a number of documents with it, we find at one place in the first document compared four variations from the standard. In the second document, at the same place, we find three of these variations repeated, and two more which are not in the first document. We count, then, nine variations; that is, the three variations common to the two documents are counted twice. In a third document, in the same place, we find all of the last three and two new ones. This gives us fourteen in all, the three being counted over again, and so on through any number of documents. In other words, " Each place where a variation occurs is counted as many times over, not only as distinct variations occur upon it, but also as the same variation occurs in different manuscripts."[2] The sum total of these variations, moreover, includes even the unique

Mode of counting variations.

---

[1] See Nestle, *Einführung in das Griechische Neue Testament*, 23.

[2] Dr. Warfield, *Textual Criticism of the New Testament*, 13.

reading of a single inferior document and the trifling variations in spelling.[1]

The work of the textual critic is to push back, as nearly as possible, to the author's own draft, and to present the *ipsissima verba* of his text. His method is to trace the various readings to their sources, to date and classify the sources, to ascertain which of these classes or families most nearly approaches the autograph, and to weigh the reasons which are most likely to have determined different readings.[2]

Work and method of the textual critic.

---

[1] The vast number of variations furnishes no cause for alarm to the devout reader of the New Testament. It is the natural result of the great number of documentary sources. A very small proportion of the variations materially affects the sense, a much smaller proportion is really important, and no variation affects an article of faith or a moral precept. Dr. Hort reckons the amount of what can, in any sense, be called substantial variation, as hardly more than a thousandth part of the entire text. (See Westcott and Hort's *Greek Testament*, Introduction, 2.)

[2] "It is quite likely that some of the variations may have been due to changes introduced by the author himself into copies within his reach, after his manuscript had gone into circulation. These copies, circulating independently of those previously issued, would become the parents of a new family of copies, and would originate diversities from the original manuscript without any fault on the part of the transcribers" (Scrivener, *Introduction*, etc., I, 18, note).

CHAPTER II

THE MANUSCRIPTS OF THE NEW TESTAMENT

THE evidence by which the New Testament text is examined and restored is gathered from three sources: Manuscripts, Versions, and Patristic Quotations.

The earliest manuscripts of the New Testament, written on papyrus, have all perished, with the exception of a few scraps, not earlier than the earliest vellum manuscripts. All the extant manuscripts are written on vellum or parchment. Vellum was made from the skins of young calves; the common parchment from those of sheep, goats, or antelopes.

All extant New Testament manuscripts written on vellum.

The extant Greek manuscripts are mostly of late date, and contain only portions of the New Testament. They are of two classes: Uncials, or Majuscules, and Cursives, or Minuscules.

Uncials.

Uncials are written in capital letters. Each letter is formed separately, and there are no divisions between the words.[1] In form, these manuscripts resemble printed books, varying in size from large folio to octavo, and smaller. The pages contain one or two, rarely three or four, columns. Breathings and accents very rarely

---

[1] The word "uncial" is derived from *uncia*, meaning the twelfth part of anything; hence, "an ounce," "an inch." It does not mean that the letters were an inch in length. There are very small uncials, as on the papyrus rolls of Herculaneum. The term is commonly traced to Jerome (preface to Job): "Uncialibus, ut vulgo aiunt, litteris, onera magis exarata, quam codices." It is thought by some, however, that Jerome wrote "initialibus" instead of "uncialibus."

occur, unless inserted by a later hand. In the earliest manuscripts punctuation is confined to a single point here and there on a level with the top of the letters, and occasionally a small break, with or without the point, to denote a pause in the sense. Later, the single point is found indiscriminately at the head, middle, or foot of the letter. In the year 458 Euthalius, a deacon of Alexandria, published an edition of the Epistles of Paul, and soon after of the Acts and Catholic Epistles, written *stichometrically*, that is, in single lines containing only so many words as could be read, consistently with the sense, at a single inspiration.[1] This mode of writing was used long before in copying the poetical books of the Old Testament. It involved, however, a great waste of parchment, so that, in manuscripts of the New Testament, it was superseded after a few centuries by punctuation-marks. Divisions of the text were early made for various purposes. In the third century Ammonius of Alexandria prepared a Harmony of the Gospels, taking the text of Matthew as the basis,

Punctuation and stichometry.

Harmonistic divisions.

[1] Thus 1 Cor. 10 : 23–26, stichometrically in English, would read as follows : —

All things are lawful for me
but all things are not expedient
all things are lawful for me
but all things edify not
let no man his own seek
("seek," ζητειτω, divided because of lack
of space, and τειτω forms a line by itself)
but that of the other
every thing that in the shambles is
sold (πωλουμενον divided)
eat nothing ask-
ing for the sake of the
conscience
for the Lord's is the earth (κυριου abbreviated, κυ.) and the fulness of it.

and placing by its side in parallel columns the similar
passages in the other Gospels. This, of course, destroyed
the continuity of their narrative. Eusebius of Cæsarea,
in the early part of the fourth century, availing him-
**Eusebian
sections and
canons.** self of the work of Ammonius, devised a method
of comparing the parallel passages not open to this
objection. He divided the text of each Gospel into
sections, the length of which was determined solely
by their relation of parallelism or similarity to passages in one or more of the other Gospels, or by their
having no parallel. Thus, Section 8 of Matthew contains one verse, Matt. 3 : 3. This is parallel with Sec. 2
of Mark (Mk. 1 : 3), Sec. 7 of Luke, (Luke 3 : 3–6),
Sec. 10 of John (J. 1 : 23). Again, Sec. 5 of Luke
(L. 2 : 48–52) has no parallel.

These sections were then numbered consecutively
in the margin, and distributed into ten tables or
canons. Canon I contained the sections corresponding in the four Gospels; Canon II the sections corresponding in Matthew, Mark, and Luke; Canon III,
Matthew, Luke, John; Canon IV, Matthew, Mark,
John. Then canons of the sections corresponding in
two Gospels. Canon V, Matthew and Luke; Canon VI,
Matthew and Mark; Canon VII, Matthew and John;
Canon VIII, Mark and Luke; Canon IX, Luke and
John; Canon X, sections peculiar to one Gospel only.

Under the number of each section in the margin of
the several Gospels, which sections were numbered in
**Notation of
canons.** black ink, there was written in red ink the number of
the canon to which it belonged. These were tabulated. Suppose, for instance, we find in the margin
of Matt. 4 : 1, $\dfrac{\iota\epsilon'}{\beta'} = \dfrac{15}{\text{II}}$: that is to say the 15th section may be found in the 2d canon. Turning to this
canon, we find that the 15th section in Matthew corre-
sponds to the 6th section in Mark and the 15th in

Luke. Turning to the margins of Mark and Luke, we find that Sec. 6 in Mark is Mark 1 : 12, and Sec. 15 in Luke is Luke 4 : 1. Thus the harmony is : Matt. 4 : 1; Mk. 1 : 12; Luke 4 : 1.

The earliest manuscript in which the Eusebian sections and canons are found is the Sinaitic, where they were added, according to Tischendorf, by a very early hand. They are found also in Codex A. Some manuscripts have the sections without the canons.[1] **Earliest occurrence of canons.**

Another ancient mode of division, ascribed by some to Tatian, the harmonist, is the division of the Gospels into chapters called τίτλοι, because a *title* or summary of the contents of each chapter is appended to the numeral which designates it. A table of these chapters was usually prefixed to each Gospel. It is noticeable that, in each of the Gospels, the designation and enumeration begins with what should be the second section. Thus, the first title in Matthew begins with the second chapter, and is prefaced with the words περι των μαγων (about the Magi). In Mark the first title begins at 1 : 23, περι του δαιμονιζομενου (about the man possessed with a demon). In Luke, at 2 : 1, περι της απογραφης (about the enrolment). In John, at 2 : 1, περι του εν Κανα γαμου (about the marriage in Cana). The reason for this is not apparent. It has been suggested that, in the first copies, the titles at the head of each Gospel were reserved for specially splendid illumination and were forgotten; but this would not explain why the second chapter was *numbered* as the first. **"Titles."**

There may also be noticed a division of the Acts **Chapters.**

[1] The original authority on this subject is the Epistle of Eusebius to Carpianus, which may be found in Tischendorf's *New Testament*, III, 145. The canons of Eusebius are tabulated in Bagster's large type Greek Testament, and the references to them are noted in the margin of the text.

and Epistles into κεφάλαια or chapters, to answer the same purpose as the τίτλοι of the Gospels. These are of later date and of uncertain origin. They do not occur in A and C (fifth century), which exhibit the τίτλοι, the sections, and one of them (A) the canons.

They are sometimes connected with the name of Euthalius, deacon of Alexandria, the reputed author of the system of stichometry. That he used them is certain, but he probably derived them from some one else.

Modern division into chapters. Our present division into chapters is commonly ascribed to Cardinal Hugo, a Dominican monk of the thirteenth century, who used it for his Concordance of the Latin Vulgate. There are better grounds for ascribing it to Stephen Langton, Archbishop of Canterbury (*ob.* 1228).

Significance of these divisions to criticism. The presence or absence of these divisions is important in determining the date of a manuscript. Thus, in seeking to fix the date of the Codex Alexandrinus, the absence of the Euthalian divisions of the Acts and Epistles would point to a date not later than the middle of the fifth century; while the insertion of the Eusebian Canons would lead us to assign a date not earlier than the latter half of the fourth century.[1]

Cursives. Cursive manuscripts are written in smaller letters, in a running hand, the letters being connected and the words separated. In the earliest cursives the system of punctuation closely resembles that of printed books. Uncial manuscripts are the earlier, from the fourth to the ninth century; while cursives range from the ninth to the fifteenth. Some cursives are older than

---

[1] For divisions of the text, see article "Bible Text," in the Schaff-Herzog *Encyclopædia*, by O. von Gebhardt, revised and largely rewritten by Ezra Abbot. On stichometry, two articles by J. Rendel Harris, *American Journal of Philology*, 1883, p. 31, and *Stichometry*, 1893. See also Scrivener, *Introduction*, etc., I, 60–67.

some uncials. In papyrus manuscripts, however, uncial and cursive writing are found side by side from the earliest times at which Greek writing is known to us, the third century B.C. In the ninth century an ornamental style of running hand was invented, which superseded the use of uncials in books. As a general rule, the upright, square, and simple uncials indicate an earlier date. Narrow, oblong, slanting characters, ornamentation, and initial letters of larger size than the rest, are marks of later date.

The following are specimens of cursive manuscripts: —

Codex Burney, 13th century.   John 21 : 18.

Copy of Pauline Epistles, Emmanuel College, Cambridge,
12th century.   Rom. 5 : 21–6 : 7.

Before the books were gathered into one collection, they were arranged in four groups: Gospels, Acts and Catholic Epistles, Pauline Epistles, and Apocalypse. Most manuscripts contain only one, or at most two, of these groups. For the purpose of reference, uncials are distinguished by capital letters of the Latin, Greek, or Hebrew alphabets, as B, Δ, א. Cursives are desig-

Mode of designating manuscripts. nated simply by numbers, as Evan. 100, signifying "cursive manuscript of the Gospels, No. 100." If a cursive manuscript contains more than one of the groups above mentioned, it appears in different lists, and with a different number in each. Thus, a cursive of the fourteenth century, in the British Museum, containing all the four groups, is described as Evan. 498, Acts 198, P. 255, Ap. 97. An uncial like א, whose readings run through the whole New Testament, is quoted everywhere by the same letter; but B, in which the Apocalypse is wanting, is assigned to the Codex Basilianus of the Apocalypse (B_2). D, in the Gospels and Acts, designates Codex Bezæ; but in the Pauline Epistles, Codex Claromontanus (D_2). The cursive manuscripts, with a few exceptions, are rarely quoted as authorities for the text. Their importance is chiefly in showing which of two readings, where the leading uncials are divided, has been adopted in the great mass of later copies.

In the whole number of manuscripts must be included the Lectionaries. The ordinary manuscripts

Lectionaries. were often adapted for church service by marking the beginning and end of each lesson with a note in the margin, indicating the time and occasion for reading it, and by prefixing to them a *Synaxarion*, or table of lessons in their order; sometimes also a *Menologion*, or calendar of the immovable festivals and the saints' days, with their appropriate lessons. Separate collections were also made of lessons from the New Testament prescribed to be read during the church year. These lessons are arranged in chronological order, without regard to their places in the New Testament, like the Gospels and Epistles in the Book of Common Prayer. Lectionaries containing lessons from the Gospels were called εὐαγγελιστάρια or, popularly, εὐαγγέλια. Those containing lessons from the Acts and Epistles were termed ἀπόστολοι or πραξαπόστολοι. A few, containing lessons from both the Gospels and the Acts and Epistles, were styled ἀποστολοευαγγέλια. The uncial character was, in some cases, retained in these collections, after cursive writing had become common, so that it is not always easy to fix their date without other indications ; but the most of the Lectionaries are in the cursive character. There are no extant Lectionaries in Greek earlier than the eighth century, or earlier than the sixth century in Syriac ; but the lectionary system is much older. Their evidence is especially important in determining the canonicity of a passage, since it is the evidence, not of individuals, but of churches, and shows that the church in a certain district believed the passage to be a part of inspired Scripture.

As parchment was a costly material, an old manu-   **Palimpsests.** script was often used for the second time, the original writing being erased by means of a sponge, a knife, or a piece of pumice-stone, and new matter written over it. Such manuscripts are called Palimpsests, or Codices Rescripti. A parchment was sometimes used three times over.[1] It has been found possible, by the application of chemicals, to restore the letters of the original manuscript. A notable instance is the restora-   **A notable** tion of Codex Ephraemi (C), in the National Library   **palimpsest.** at Paris, in which the works of the Syrian Father,

[1] See Scrivener, *Introduction*, etc., I, 141.

Ephraem, were written over the original New Testament text. The original writing was brought to light by the librarian, Carl Hase, in 1834–35, by the application of the Giobertine tincture (prussiate of potash). It was edited by Tischendorf in 1843–45.[1]

We shall notice the five primary uncials, so called from their age and importance.

Codex Sinaiticus (א).

Codex Sinaiticus (א): probably about the middle of the fourth century. Now in the Imperial Library at St. Petersburg. It was discovered by Tischendorf in 1859, in the Convent of St. Catherine on Mt. Sinai.

The story of its discovery.

The following is Tischendorf's own description of the discovery. "On the afternoon of this day (Feb. 7, 1859) I was taking a walk with the steward of the convent in the neighborhood, and as we returned toward sunset, he begged me to take some refreshment with him in his cell. Scarcely had he entered the room when, resuming our former subject of conversation, he said, ' And I, too, have read a Septuagint; ' and so saying he took down from the corner of the room a bulky kind of volume wrapped up in a red cloth, and laid it before me. I unrolled the cover, and discovered, to my great surprise, not only those very fragments which, fifteen years before, I had taken out of the basket, but also other parts of the Old Testament, the New Testament complete, and, in addition, the Epistle of Barnabas, and a part of the *Pastor* of

---

[1] On palimpsests, see Scrivener, *Introduction*, etc., I, 25, 141; Tischendorf, *New Testament*, III, 366; Mrs. Agnes Lewis, *The Four Gospels translated from the Sinaitic Palimpsest.* For a full description of the New Testament manuscripts, the reader will consult the Prolegomena to Tischendorf's larger eighth edition of his Greek Testament, in the third volume, prepared by Dr. Caspar R. Gregory, and Scrivener's *Introduction to the Criticism of the New Testament*, I. A compendious description will be found in the Schaff-Herzog *Encyclopædia*, article "Bible Text," by von Gebhardt.

SPECIMEN OF A PROOF OF THE FACSIMILE EDITION OF CODEX SINAITICUS א.

Hermas. Full of joy, which this time I had the self-command to conceal from the steward and the rest of the community, I asked, as if in a careless way, for permission to take the manuscript into my sleeping-chamber to look it over more at leisure. . . . I knew that I held in my hand the most precious biblical treasure in existence — a document whose age and importance exceeded that of all the manuscripts which I had ever examined during twenty years' study of the subject. . . . Though my lamp was dim and the night cold, I sat down at once to transcribe the Epistle of Barnabas. For two centuries search has been made in vain for the original Greek of the first part of this Epistle, which has been known only through a very faulty Latin translation. And yet this letter, from the end of the second down to the beginning of the fourth century, had an extensive authority, since many Christians assigned to it and to the *Pastor* of Hermas a place side by side with the inspired writings of the New Testament. This was the very reason why these two writings were both thus bound up with the Sinaitic Bible, the transcription of which is to be referred to the first half of the fourth century and about the time of the first Christian emperor." [1]

The New Testament text of the Sinaitic Codex is complete. The original text has been corrected in many places. The Eusebian sections are indicated in the margin of the Gospels in a hand evidently contemporaneous with the text. The Codex is $13\frac{1}{2}$ inches broad by $14\frac{7}{8}$ inches high, and consists of $346\frac{1}{2}$ leaves of beautiful vellum, of which 199 contain portions of the Septuagint Version, and $147\frac{1}{2}$ the New Testament, the Epistle of Barnabas, and the fragment of the Shepherd of Hermas. Each page has four col-

Character of the codex.

[1] See further under Tischendorf in the history of the printed text.

C

umns, with forty-eight lines in each column. The poetical books of the Old Testament, being written stichometrically, admit of only two columns on a page. In the order of the books, Paul's Epistles precede the Acts. The Epistle to the Hebrews stands with the Pauline letters and follows 2 Thessalonians. There are no breathings or accents, and marks of punctuation are scanty. Words are divided at the end of a line, as the κ from ου in οὐκ. The numerous corrections which disfigure the Codex are mostly due to later hands of the sixth and seventh centuries and later. A few appear to have been made by the original scribe.

Codex Vaticanus (B).   Codex Vaticanus (B). Fourth century. Generally regarded as slightly older than א. It is in the Vatican Library at Rome. Contains the Septuagint Version of the Old Testament, with some gaps, and the New Testament to Hebrews 9 : 14, inclusive. The Pastoral Epistles, Philemon, and the Apocalypse are lost. The Catholic Epistles had followed the Acts. It is a quarto volume, arranged in quires of five sheets or ten leaves each, and is written on thin vellum made of the skins of antelopes. It is 10½ inches high, 10 inches broad, and 4½ thick. It has three columns to a page, except in the poetical books of the Old Testament, which are written stichometrically, and in which there are two columns to a page. Its antiquity is attested by the absence of divisions into κεφάλαια and of sections and canons, instead of which it has a scheme of chapters or sections of its own, which seem to have been formed for the purpose of reference. A

Divisions of the text in B.   new section always begins where there is some break in the sense, and many of those in the Gospels consist of but one of our modern verses. The Gospel of Matthew contains 170 of these divisions, Mark 62, Luke 152, and John 80. In the Acts are two sets of sections, thirty-six longer and in an older hand, sixty-

PLATE II

SPECIMEN OF THE CODEX VATICANUS, SHOWING THE END OF MATTHEW AND BEGINNING OF MARK

(Half of a page, of which the full size, not including margins, is 10 in. × 10½ in.)

nine smaller and more recent. Each of these also begins after a break in the sense; but they are quite independent of each other, as a larger section will sometimes commence in the middle of a smaller, the latter not being a subdivision of the former. In the Catholic Epistles and in the Pauline Epistles there are two sets of sections, but in the Epistles the older sections are the more numerous. The breathings and accents have been added by a later hand, according to Tischendorf and Hort, of the tenth or eleventh century. This hand appears to have traced the faint lines of the original writing; and the writer, being anxious at the same time to represent a critical revision of the text, left untouched such words or letters as he wished to reject. These untouched places enable us to see the Codex in its primitive condition.

Attempts to examine and collate this codex were for many years baffled by the custodians of the Vatican Library and the authorities of the Roman Church.[1] Roman Catholic scholars undertook the work which they refused to allow others to do. An edition by Cardinal Mai was issued in 1857, but it was full of faults, so that it never could be used with confidence. A grudging and limited permission to Tischendorf to consult the Codex enabled him to issue, in 1867, an edition superior to any that had preceded it. The edition of the New Testament by Vercellone and Cozza appeared in 1868, and was complete and critical, though not without errors. A splendid edition was issued in 1889, under the care of Abbate Cozza-Luzi, in which the entire text was exhibited in photograph.   *Editions of B.*

Codex Alexandrinus (A). Fifth century. In the British Museum, where it was placed at the founda-   *Codex Alexandrinus (A).*

[1] See under Tischendorf and Tregelles in the history of the printed text.

tion of the library of that institution in 1753, having previously belonged to the king's private collection from the year 1628, when it was sent by Cyril Lucar, Patriarch of Constantinople, as a gift to Charles I. An old Arabic inscription on the first leaf states that it was written by the hand of Thecla the Martyr. The Codex is bound in four volumes, three of which contain the Septuagint Version of the Old Testament with some gaps, amounting to nearly six hundred verses. The fourth volume contains the New Testament. The whole of Matthew's Gospel to 25 : 6 is missing, together with John 6 : 50–8 : 52, and 2 Cor. 4 : 13–12 : 6. After the Apocalypse is found what was until very recently the only known extant copy of the first or genuine Epistle of Clement of Rome, and a small fragment of a second of suspected authenticity. It would appear that these two Epistles were designed to form a part of the volume of Scripture, being represented in the table of contents under the head H KAINH ΔΙΑΘΗΚΗ. To these are added the eighteen Psalms of Solomon as distinct from Scripture.

Character of the codex. The Codex is in quarto, $12\frac{3}{4}$ inches high and $10\frac{1}{4}$ broad, and consists of 773 leaves. Each page contains two columns of fifty or fifty-one lines each. The uncials are of an elegant but simple form, in a uniform hand, though in some places larger than in others. The punctuation, which no later hand has meddled with, consists merely of a point placed at the end of a sentence, usually on a level with the top of the preceding letter. A vacant space follows the point at the end of a paragraph, the space being proportioned to the break in the sense. Capital letters

Capitalization and divisions of A. of various sizes, written in common ink, are found at the beginning of books and sections. These capitals stand in the margin entirely outside of the column; so that if the section begins in the middle of a line, the capital is postponed until the beginning of the next line, the first letter of which is always the capital, even though it be in the middle of a word. The first line of Mark, the first three of Luke, the first verse of John, the opening of the Acts down to δι, and so on for other books, are in vermilion.

This is the first Codex which has κεφάλαια proper, the Ammonian sections and the Eusebian canons complete.

Codex Ephraemi (C). Fifth century. In the National Library at Paris. It was brought into France by Catherine de' Medici. It is a palimpsest, the ancient writing having been removed about the twelfth century in order to transcribe the works of Ephraem, the Syrian Father. An attempt to recover the original writing by the application of a chemical preparation, in 1834, defaced the vellum with stains of various colors. The older writing was first noticed nearly two centuries ago. A collation of the New Testament was made by Wetstein in 1716 ; but the first thorough collation was by Tischendorf in 1843. Codex Ephraemi (C).

The Codex originally contained the whole Greek Bible. Only sixty-four leaves remain of the Old Testament. Of the New Testament ninety-three leaves are missing. Those which remain contain portions of every book except 1 Thessalonians and 2 John. There is but one column to a page, containing from forty to forty-six lines. The characters are larger and more elaborate than those of A or B. The punctuation resembles that of A. The Ammonian sections stand in the margin, but the chemical applications have not revealed the Eusebian canons. These canons were commonly noted in vermilion, and lines of the text written in vermilion have been completely obliterated. There is no trace of chapters in the Acts, Epistles, or Apocalypse. In the Gospels the Contents of C.

κεφάλαια are not placed in the upper margin of the page as in A, but a list of their τίτλοι preceded each Gospel. Two correctors have handled the Codex, possibly of the sixth and ninth centuries.

Codex Bezæ (D).

Codex Bezæ or Cantabrigiensis (D). Sixth century. In the Library of the University of Cambridge. It is named from Theodore Beza, who presented it to the University in 1581. It contains only the Gospels and Acts, and is the first example of a copy in two languages, giving a Latin version in addition to the Greek text. It is marked by numerous interpolations and departures from the normal text, and on this account some critics refuse to place it among the primary uncials. It originally contained the Catholic Epistles between the Gospels and the Acts, and in the Latin translation a few verses of 3 John remain, followed by the words "Epistulæ Johannis iii explicit, incipit actus Apostolorum," as if the Epistle of Jude were displaced or wanting. It is a quarto volume, ten inches high and eight broad, with one column on a page, the Greek text being on the left-hand page, and the Latin facing it on the right. There are thirty-three lines on every page, the matter being arranged stichometrically. It has not the Eusebian canons, but only the Ammonian sections. It has suffered at the hands of nine or ten different revisers. The margins of the church lessons for Saturday and Sunday contain liturgical notes in thick

Divisions of D.

letters. A few others for the great feasts and fast days occur, and, in a hand of about the twelfth century, lessons for the festivals of St. George and St. Dionysius, the patron saints of England and France.[1]

[1] Among the secondary uncials the most important are: D₂, Codex Claromontanus, second half of the sixth century, National Library at Paris, Greek and Latin, contains the Pauline Epistles and the Epistle to the Hebrews. E₂, sixth century, Codex Lau-

PLATE III

A SPECIMEN OF THE CODEX EPHRAEMI

(Original size of page, 12¼ in. × 9¼ in. ; of the part reproduced, 7¼ in. × 9 in.)

Reproduced by permission from F. G. Kenyon's *Our Bible and the Ancient MSS.*, Eyre &

dianus, Bodleian Library at Oxford, Greek and Latin, contains the Acts. L, Codex Regius, eighth century, National Library at Paris, contains the Gospels complete : a very ancient text. Tᵃ, Codex Borgianus, fifth century, Propaganda at Rome, Greek and Coptic, contains 179 verses of Luke and John. Dr. Hort ranks it next after B and א for excellence of text. Z, Codex Dublinensis, palimpsest, sixth century, Trinity College, Dublin, contains 295 verses of Matthew, in twenty-two fragments ; agrees with א rather than with B. Δ, Codex Sangallensis, ninth century, library of the monastery of St. Gall in the northeast of Switzerland, Gospels nearly complete ; a Latin interlinear translation. The text in Mark is of the same type as L. Ξ, Codex Zacynthius, eighth century, palimpsest, in the Library of the British and Foreign Bible Society in London, contains 342 verses of Luke's Gospel. Dr. Hort places it next to Tᵃ. A continuous commentary by different authors (catena) accompanies the text. Scrivener says this is the earliest known — indeed, the only — uncial furnished with a catena.

CHAPTER III

VERSIONS

Versions.

VERSIONS of the New Testament writings were demanded early by the rapid spread of the Gospel to the Syrians, Egyptians, and the Latin-speaking people of Africa, Italy, and the west of Europe. Translations into Syriac and Latin were made in the second century, and later into Coptic, when Alexander's conquest opened Egypt.

Worth of versions in textual criticism.

Versions are important in textual criticism because they are earlier than extant manuscripts, because their ages are known, and because they are, generally, authorised translations, made either by a body of men, or by a single recognised and accepted authority. Versions may indeed have suffered in the course of transmission, but when the ancient versions accord, it is reasonable to conclude that in such passages they have not suffered.

On the other hand, their evidence is less direct than that of manuscripts, since we must translate them back into their originals in any case of doubt. They have been transmitted in manuscripts, just as the Greek original has been, and are liable to the same accidents which have affected the Greek text. They have undergone similar textual corruptions. No manuscript copy of a version is earlier than the fourth century. Therefore it may be found as difficult to arrive at the primitive text of a version as of the Greek original. Some versions, moreover, are second-

24

ary, derived from other versions of the Greek; and some merely give the sense, without attempting verbal renderings.

Versions by themselves, therefore, cannot establish any reading. They can only supplement manuscript evidence. If an ancient version accords with a very early Greek manuscript in some particular reading, the evidence is weighty as to the early prevalence of that reading; and if this testimony is supported by a second version, its weight is greatly increased. If we are sure of the original words of a Syriac or Latin translation, we may have a reasonably correct idea of the words of a Greek text extant in the first half of the second century. On the omission of words and clauses the testimony of versions is as clear as that of original manuscripts. It must be noted, further, that the value of a version's evidence at certain points will depend somewhat on the character of the language into which the Greek is rendered. For instance, a Latin version would seldom testify to the presence or absence of the Greek article.

Office of versions in criticism.

1. **Latin Versions.** — A comparison of the Old Latin texts, previous to Jerome's version, indicates that they all are offshoots from one, or at most two, parent stocks.

Latin versions.

One of the several recensions current toward the end of the fourth century was known as Itala. It was for a long time thought that it originated in Africa in the second half of the second century.[1]

Three groups of Old Latin manuscripts are recognised, each representing a distinct type of text: (1) African, agreeing generally with quotations in Ter-

---

[1] See Cardinal Wiseman, *Two Lectures on Some Parts of the Controversy concerning 1 John 5 : 7.* Republished in *Essays on Various Subjects*, I, 1853, Rome. Later scholarship has become less confident as to the African origin.

Jerome's revision.

tullian and Cyprian; (2) European, either independent or based on the African; (3) Italian, formed on the European type, and revised with the aid of later Greek manuscripts. Many of the Old Latin manuscripts, however, present texts which cannot be assigned to either of these classes. At the end of the fourth century there was so much variation in existing texts that Jerome was requested by Pope Damasus to undertake a revision. His labour was expended chiefly on the Old Testament. In all parts of the New Testament, except the Gospels, his revision was cursory. The texts which precede his version remain to us only in fragments, and are to be gathered, largely, from citations by the Fathers. These patristic citations may be found, not only in writings composed before Jerome, but also in later compositions, since a long time elapsed before Jerome's work obtained general currency. Down to the end of the sixth century different texts were used at the writer's pleasure. Accordingly we find in some exclusively an old text, in others only Jerome's version, while others again employ both.[1]

[1] Some idea of the differences may be gained from the following parallels, the variations from Jerome's version being designated by italics: —

Romans 10:9

JEROME	IRENÆUS	HILARY OF POITIERS
quia si confitearis in ore tuo Dominum Jesum, et in corde tuo credideris quod Deus illum suscitavit a mortuis, salvus eris.	*quoniam* si confitearis in ore tuo Dominum Jesum et *credideris in corde tuo quoniam* Deus illum *excitavit* a mortuis, salvus eris.	quia si *confessus fueris* in ore tuo, *quia Dominus Jesus est*, et credideris in corde tuo, *quia* Deus illum suscitavit a mortuis, *salvaberis*.

Romans 13:6

JEROME	IRENÆUS	AUGUSTINE
Ideo enim et tributa præstatis; ministri enim Dei sunt, in hoc ipsum servientes.	*Propter hoc* enim et tributa *penditis;* ministri enim Dei sunt in hoc ipsum servientes.	Ideo (elsewhere propter hoc) enim et tributa præstatis; ministri enim Dei in hoc ipsum *perseverantes*.

A second revision was attempted by Alcuin (735–804), and a third by Sixtus V (1590). The modern authorised Vulgate is the Clementine (1592), which is substantially Jerome's version. The Old Latin version of the New Testament was translated directly from the original Greek. The Vulgate was only a revision of the Old Latin. But the Old Latin was made long before any of our existing Greek manuscripts, and takes us back almost to within a generation of the time at which the New Testament books were composed. The Old Latin Version is therefore one of the most interesting and valuable evidences which we possess for the condition of the New Testament text in the earliest times.[1]

Value of the Old Latin Version.

Philippians 2 : 7

JEROME	TERTULLIAN	NOVATIAN
sed semet ipsum exinanivit, formam servi accipiens, in similitudinem hominum factus et habitu inventus ut homo.	*exhausit* semet ipsum *accepta effigie* servi *et* in *similitudine hominis et figura* inventus ut homo.	semet ipsum exinanivit formam servi accipiens, in *similitudine* hominum factus et habitu inventus ut homo.

Titus 2 : 6–8

JEROME	LUCIFER OF CAGLIARI	AMBROSIASTER
Juvenes similiter hortare, ut sobrii sint. In omnibus te ipsum præbe exemplum bonorum operum, in doctrina, in integritate, in gravitate, in sermone sano et irreprehensibili, ut is qui ex adverso est vereatur, nihil habens malum dicere de nobis.	Juvenes similiter hortare, ut sobrii sint in omnibus, (note difference of punctuation,) *per omnia* te ipsum *formam præbens* bonorum operum in doctrina (punctuation), in integritate, in gravitate, in sermone *sanum, irreprehensibilem*, ut *adversarius revereatur* nihil habens *quid* dicere malum de nobis.	*Juniores* similiter hortare, *continentes esse per omnia, temet* ipsum *præbens* exemplum bonorum operum in doctrina, in integritate, in gravitate, *verbum sanum, irreprehensibile*, ut is qui e *diverso* est *revereatur* nihil habens dicere de nobis *dignum reprehensione*.

[1] On Latin Versions, see: H. Rönsch, *Das N. T. Tertullians*, etc., Leipzig, 1871. Id. *Itala und Vulgata*, 2 Ausg., Marburg, 1875. Wordsworth and White, *Novum Testamentum Latine*, Oxford, 1887. Wordsworth, White, and Sanday, *Old Latin Biblical Texts*, Oxford, 1888. F. C. Burkitt, *The Old Latin and*

Syriac versions.

2. Syriac Versions.—The gospel was first preached in the East. The nearness of Syria to Judæa, and the early growth of the church at Antioch and Damascus, must have produced an early demand for a rendering into the Syriac tongue. Of extant versions there are five: Peshitto, Curetonian, Philoxenian and Harclean, Jerusalem or Palestinian, and the Lewis Palimpsest.

The Peshitto.

The Peshitto is the great standard version of the Syriac church, made not later than the third century. It is known to us in 177 manuscripts, most of which are in the British Museum. Two of these are of the fifth century; at least a dozen more not later than the sixth century. The Peshitto does not contain those books of the New Testament which were the last to be generally accepted, as 2 Peter, 2 and 3 John, Jude, and the Apocalypse.

The Peshitto a revision.

About the beginning of the present century Griesbach and Hug asserted that the Peshitto was not the original Syriac, but a revision of an earlier version. In 1842 eighty leaves of a copy of the Gospels in Syriac were discovered in the Syrian Convent of St. Mary in the Nitrian Desert. These contained a different text from those of any manuscripts previously known. They were edited by Dr. Cureton of the British Museum, who maintained that they exhibited the very words of the Lord's discourses in the language in which they were originally spoken. The manuscript is of the fifth century, practically contemporary with the earliest existing manuscripts of

The Curetonian.

the Itala, Cambridge Texts and Studies, IV, 3, Cambridge, 1896. S. Berger, *Histoire de la Vulgate pendant les premiers siècles du Moyen Age,* Paris, 1893. D. F. Fritzsche, article " Lateinische Bibelübersetzungen," in Herzog's *Real-Encyklopädie.* On the Vetus Latina of Paul's Epistles: Ziegler, *Die Lateinischen Bibelübersetzungen vor Hieronymus,* München, 1879.

the Peshitto. Cureton, however, argued that the character of the translation showed that its original must have been earlier than the original of the Peshitto, and that the Peshitto was the revision of the Old Syriac.[1]

Cureton's view has been hotly contested. The question is, whether the Curetonian, which is less accurate, scholarly, and smooth than the Peshitto, is a corruption of the latter, or whether, as Cureton maintained, the Peshitto is a revision of the Curetonian. It may be said that it is unlikely that an accurate version like the Peshitto should have been deliberately altered for the worse, and that a less accurate, independent version should have passed into circulation. The affinities of the Curetonian version are with the older forms of the Greek text, while those of the Peshitto are with its later forms. Tischendorf assigns the Curetonian to the middle, the Peshitto to the end, of the second century. Others assign the Peshitto to the end of the third or beginning of the fourth. Dr. Hort says that the Curetonian text is not only itself a valuable authority, but renders the comparatively late and revised character of the Peshitto a matter of certainty.

Various opinions as to the Curetonian.

The question was reopened by the discovery, in 1892, by Mrs. Agnes Lewis, in the Convent of St. Catherine on Mt. Sinai, of a Syriac palimpsest of the four Gospels. The following is Mrs. Lewis's own account of her discovery:[2] —

The Lewis palimpsest.

"In the Convent of St. Catherine, on Mt. Sinai, a chest containing ancient Syriac manuscripts has lain

---

[1] The manuscript of the Curetonian Syriac Gospels contains Matt. 1-8 : 22 ; 10 : 31-23 : 25. Of Mark, 16 : 17-20. Of John, 1 : 1-42 ; 3 : 6-7 : 37, and fragments of 14 : 11-29. Of Luke, 2 : 48-3 : 16 ; 7 : 33-15 : 21 ; 17 : 24-24 : 44.

[2] *The Four Gospels translated from the Sinaitic Palimpsest*, London, 1894.

undisturbed for centuries. Professor Palmer saw its contents in 1868, and thus refers to them: 'Among a pile of patristic and other works of no great age or interest are some curious old Syriac books, and one or two palimpsests. My hurried visit prevented me from examining these with any great care; but they would no doubt well repay investigation.'

First examination of the palimpsest.

"The first real examination of these books was reserved for Mr. Rendel Harris, who, in 1889, after a stay of fifteen days at the Convent, contrived to disarm all prejudices, and to obtain access to these hidden treasures. . . .

"Amongst the ancient volumes which were produced for our inspection by the late Hegoumenos and Librarian, Father Galakteon, was a thick volume, whose leaves had evidently been unturned for centuries, as they could be separated only by manipulation with the fingers, and in some cases only by the steam of a kettle. A single glance told me that the book was a palimpsest, and I soon ascertained that the upper writing was a very entertaining account of the lives of women saints, and that its date was, as I then read it, a thousand and nine years after Alexander, that is, A.D. 697. After the word 'nine' there is a small hole in the vellum, which, as Mr. Rendel Harris believes, occupies the place of the syllable corresponding to the 'ty' of 'ninety,' and the date is thus probably A.D. 778.

"I then examined the more ancient writing which lay beneath this. It is in two columns, one of which is always projected onto the margin, and it is written in the same character, but in a much smaller hand than the later writing which covers it. It was also slightly reddish in colour. As I glanced down the margin for over 280 pages, every word that I could decipher was from the Gospels, and so were the lines which at the top or bottom of several pages were free of the later writing. And few, indeed, were the pages which had not a distinct title, such as 'Evangelium,' 'da Mathai,' 'da Marcus,' or 'da Luca.'"

Mrs. Lewis photographed the pages which were shown to the late Professor Bensley, who was then engaged on a critical edition of the Curetonian Gospels. He pronounced the text to be of the same type as the Curetonian. *The work of Mrs. Lewis.*

A second expedition to the Sinaitic convent was organised, in which Mrs. Lewis was accompanied by Professor Bensley, J. Rendel Harris, and F. C. Burkitt. In forty days the text of the Gospels was transcribed directly from the manuscript, and Mrs. Lewis succeeded in restoring much of the faded writing by means of a chemical agent.

The manuscript is written on strong vellum. The text of the Gospels underlies about 284 pages on 142 leaves of the Martyrology. In addition to these leaves the scribe made use of four leaves from a fourth-century manuscript of the Gospels, many leaves from a volume of Syriac apocrypha, containing the Acts of Thomas and the Repose of Mary, and other leaves from a Greek manuscript, not identified. *Appearance of the manuscript.*

The text presents a number of variations from the standard Greek text, but most of them are curious and interesting rather than important. There are some transpositions, as in John 18, where the questioning by the High Priest follows immediately upon Christ's being led to him, and Peter's three denials are grouped in a consecutive narrative in the succeeding verses. In Luke 22 there is a fresh arrangement of the narrative from ver. 17 to ver. 21, by which it is made more compact and orderly. The interpolation at Luke 23: 48, which occurs only in Codex Bezæ, appears here: "Woe unto us, what hath befallen us? Woe unto us *Variations of the manuscript.*

for our sins." Matt. 1 : 16 reads, "Joseph begat Jesus who is called Christ," and in ver. 25 the words "and knew her not until" are omitted. Yet Matt. 1 : 18 is retained, "When they had not come near to one another, she was found with child of the Holy Ghost." The last twelve verses of Mark are omitted.

Relations to other Syriac Versions. The question of the relation of this Codex to other Syriac Versions is far too technical to be discussed here. An important point is the relation of the Curetonian Version to the Diatessaron or Gospel Harmony of Tatian, composed about 160 A.D., and which was charged with omitting whatever went to show that Jesus was born of the seed of David according to the flesh. The whole problem presents the following factors: (1) An early Syriac Version represented by the Curetonian, but how early? (2) The Peshitto. Is it a revision of an earlier version, and if so, is that version the Curetonian? (3) Tatian's Diatessaron. Was it originally written in Syriac? Was it earlier than the Curetonian? To quote Mrs. Lewis, "Was the Diatessaron compiled in the second century from the version contained in the Curetonian and in the Sinai Codices, or did that version come into existence only in the fourth century, when the use of the Diatessaron was discontinued?" (4) The Lewis Palimpsest. It is no doubt earlier than the Peshitto. Is it earlier than the Curetonian? It does not perfectly coincide with the Curetonian. Eb. Nestle and J. Rendel Harris both hold that it represents the very first attempt to render the Gospel into Syriac, and thus both the Diatessaron and the Curetonian are revisions of it.[1]

---

[1] See G. Salmon, *Some Criticism of the Text of the New Testament,* 75.

On Syriac Versions, see : Th. Zahn, *Geschichte der neutesta-mentlichen Kanons,* Leipzig, 1888, 1891. Eb. Nestle, article "Syrische Bibelübersetzungen," in Herzog's *Real-Encyklopädie;*

The Philoxenian Version was made by Philoxenus, Bishop of Mabug (Hierapolis) in Eastern Syria, in 508; probably with a view to provide a more literal version than the Peshitto. Few traces of it, in its original form, remain.[1]

Improperly confounded with the Philoxenian is a version made at Alexandria, in 616, by Thomas of Harkel, also Bishop of Mabug. It was formerly regarded as a revision of the Philoxenian; but the opinion has gained ground that it was substantially a new version. It is known as the Harclean Syriac, and is characterised by slavish adherence to the Greek, even to the destruction of the Syriac idiom.

Philoxenian and Harclean Syriac.

The Jerusalem Syriac exists only in fragments, and differs in dialect from all the other versions. It is believed to have been made in the fifth or sixth century, and to have been used exclusively in Palestine. It was discovered at the end of the last century in the Vatican Library, and was edited in 1861-64. Since

Jerusalem and Karkaphensian Syriac.

full catalogue of literature. Baethgen, *Evangelienfragmente. Der griechische Text des Curetonschen Syrers wiederhergestellt*, Leipzig, 1885. G. H. Gwilliam, The Material for the Criticism of the Peshitto New Testament, *Studia Biblica*, Oxford, 1891, III, 47-104. R. L. Bensley, J. Rendel Harris, F. C. Burkitt, *The Four Gospels in Syriac, transcribed from the Sinaitic Palimpsest*, Cambridge, 1894. Agnes Smith Lewis, *The Four Gospels translated from the Syriac of the Sinaitic Palimpsest*, London, 1894. Tischendorf, *New Testament*, III, 806 ff.; list of earlier articles on the Curetonian Syriac. Scrivener, *Introduction*, etc., II, 6 ff.

On Tatian's Diatessaron, see A. Harnack, *Geschichte der altchristlichen Litteratur*, Th. I, S. 485 ff. J. Hamlyn Hill, *The Earliest Life of Christ, being the Diatessaron of Tatian*, Clarks, Edinburgh, 1894.

[1] Unless the manuscript brought to light by Dr. Isaac H. Hall of New York, in 1876, can be shown, as is claimed, to be the unrevised Philoxenian. This manuscript is now in the library of Union Theological Seminary, New York.

D

then fragments of the Gospels and Acts have been found in the British Museum and at St. Petersburg, and two additional lectionaries and fragments of the Pauline Epistles in the Bodleian at Oxford and at Mt. Sinai. Two more lectionaries have been discovered at Mt. Sinai by Mrs. Lewis.[1]

What is called the Karkaphensian Syriac is not a continuous version, but a collection of passages on which annotations have been made, dealing with questions of spelling and pronunciation.

Egyptian versions.

3. Egyptian Versions. — The language used by the natives of Egypt at the time when the Bible was first translated for their use, is called Coptic. It was allied to the Demotic or vulgar language, so called to distinguish it from the Hieratic or priestly language. The Demotic writing contained a mixture of alphabetic signs, each of which represented a single sound, with other signs representing syllables, and others not phonetic but pictorial. With the entrance of Christianity into Egypt a new and strictly phonetic alphabet was introduced, the characters being adopted from the Greek alphabet.

Three Egyptian Versions.

We are acquainted with five Egyptian Versions, of which only three need be mentioned: the Memphitic or Bahiric; the Thebaic or Sahidic; the Bashmuric. The Memphitic was current in Northern Egypt. It was the most literary dialect of the Egyptian language, and is the Coptic of to-day, so far as the language still exists. Only in the Bahiric are complete copies of the New Testament still extant. All the other Coptic versions exist only in fragments. The oldest and best manuscript (Oxford, Gospels) is of the latter part of the twelfth century. It is a good and careful trans-

[1] See J. Rendel Harris, *Biblical Fragments from Mt. Sinai.* G. H. Gwilliam, *Anecdota Oxoniensia*, Semitic Series, I, 5, 1893; 9, 1896.

lation. It did not originally include the Apocalypse. The Thebaic was current in Southern Egypt. It exists only in fragments, but these are very numerous, especially at Paris. The fragments, if combined, would compose a nearly complete New Testament, with considerable portions of the Old Testament. It is probably later than the Bahiric. The language is less polished, and the text not so pure. The Bashmuric was an adaptation of the Thebaic, in the dialect of herdsmen living in the Nile Delta. Only a few fragments remain, covering about three hundred verses of the Fourth Gospel, and five verses of the Pauline Epistles.

For the Æthiopic, Armenian, and Gothic Versions, the reader may consult Tischendorf's New Testament, III, and Scrivener's "Introduction," etc. A tenth-century manuscript of the Armenian version is interesting as containing the last twelve verses of Mark's Gospel, with a heading stating that they are "of the Elder Aristion." One Aristion is mentioned by Papias as having been a disciple of the Lord.

If the writer of these verses could be identified without doubt as a disciple of the Lord, the fact would naturally have an important bearing on the much-vexed question of the authenticity of the passage. But such identification is far from positive.[1]

Æthiopic, Armenian, and Gothic Versions.

The Elder Aristion.

[1] See Eusebius, H. E., III, 39.

The Gothic Version of the Gospels may be seen in Bosworth and Waring's *Gothic and Anglo-Saxon Gospels in Parallel Columns.* For an interesting treatment of Ulfilas, the author of the Gothic Version, see T. Hodgkin, *Italy and her Invaders*, I, Pt. I, 80 ff.

On Egyptian Versions, see J. B. Lightfoot, in Scrivener's *Introduction*, 4th ed. II, 91–144. Tischendorf, Prolegomena, 859 ff.

CHAPTER IV

PATRISTIC QUOTATIONS

THE third source of textual evidence is furnished by quotations from the Greek Testament by other writers, especially the Church Fathers. This class of evidence is styled "the Evidence of Patristic Quotation." It has a certain value, but the value is limited or qualified by numerous considerations. While it is probable that nearly the whole substance of New Testament teaching could be recovered from the Patristic writings, the same cannot be said of the text. The text of many of the Fathers is itself in an imperfect state. "It is a shame," says Dr. Nestle, "that the most important Fathers are not yet before us in proper editions." Dr. Sanday says: "The field of the patristic writings needs to be thoroughly overhauled. What makes this the more urgent is that where the text has not been critically tested, the quotations from the Bible are the first to suffer. The scribes were constantly in the habit of substituting the text with which they were themselves familiar for that which they found before them in the manuscript. So that what we have very frequently is, not the words of the Father as they were originally written, but simply the late Byzantine or Vulgate text current in the Middle Ages when the manuscript was copied." [1]

Imperfection of patristic texts.

[1] Expositor, 1st Ser., XI, 171. The Vienna Academy has been issuing, since 1867, a *Corpus Scriptorum Ecclesiasticorum Latinorum*, which already amounts to fifty volumes; and the

The habits of the Fathers in quotation were very loose. Having no concordances or indices, or anything resembling the modern apparatus for facilitating reference, and often no manuscript, they were frequently compelled to rely upon memory for their citations. Quoting from memory explains what we so often find, — combinations of different passages, transpositions, and sense-renderings. Though a full summary of the whole gospel life could be composed from the quotations of Justin Martyr, his quotations are careless. He quotes the same passage differently on different occasions. Although he cites written documents, he often quotes from memory, and interweaves words which are given separately by the Synoptists. He condenses, combines, and transposes the language of the Lord as recorded in the Gospel records. Take, for example, Matt. 5 : 22, 39, 40, 41, and Luke 6 : 29. In Justin, 1 Apol. XVI, we read τῷ τυπτόντι σοῦ τὴν σιαγόνα πάρεχε καὶ τὴν ἄλλην, καὶ τὸν αἴροντα σοῦ τὸν χιτῶνα ἢ τὸ ἱμάτιον μὴ κωλύσῃς. Ὃς δὲ ἂν ὀργισθῇ ἐνοχός ἐστιν εἰς τὸ πῦρ, παντὶ δὲ ἀγγαρεύοντί σε μίλιον ἀκολούθησον. Here we have several verses massed, apparently from two Evangelists. Luke is literally followed in the first nine words. The order of the Gospel is not observed, and the sense is changed in the words about the coat and the cloke.

Similarly Matt. 5 : 46; comp. Luke 6 : 27. Justin, 1 Apol. XV: εἰ ἀγαπᾶτε τοὺς ἀγαπῶντας ὑμᾶς, τί καινὸν ποιεῖτε; καὶ γὰρ οἱ πόρνοι τοῦτο ποιοῦσιν. Here, instead of "What reward have ye?" Justin has "What new thing do ye do?" For "publicans" he gives "fornicators."

Again, see Clement of Alexandria, Strom. III, 4, 36, where Matt. 5 : 16 is given τὰ ἀγαθὰ ὑμῶν ἔργα λαμψάτω, "Let your good works shine."

Berlin Academy has in process an edition of the *Ante-Nicene Church Teachers.*

Patristic habits in quotation.

Apostolic
Fathers not
valuable in
Scripture
quotation.

The Apostolic Fathers are of little value for patristic quotation, since they do not so much quote as blend the language of the New Testament with their own. Fragments of most of the canonical Epistles are embedded in their writings, and their diction is more or less coloured by that of the apostolic books,[1] and different passages are combined.[2]

It is possible that, in some cases, the writers do not intend to quote, but merely to use the words loosely

Inaccurate
citation.

by way of allusion. But often, even when quotation is intended, the citation is inaccurate. To take a single instance, Clement of Rome was familiar with the Epistle to the Hebrews, and references to it occur frequently in his letter to the Corinthians; but in his citation of Heb. 1 : 3, 4, in Ch. 36, for δόξης "glory,"

---

[1] For example, see Ignatius, Magn. X, ὑπέρθεσθε οὖν τὴν κακὴν ζύμην τὴν παλαιωθεῖσαν καὶ ἐνοξίσασαν, καὶ μεταβάλεσθε εἰς νέαν ζύμην ὅς ἐστιν Ἰησοῦς Χριστός, " Put away the vile leaven which hath waxed stale and sour, and betake yourselves to the new leaven which is Jesus Christ." Compare 1 Cor. 5 : 7.

Ignatius to Polycarp, I, πάντων ἀνέχου ἐν ἀγάπῃ, "Suffer all in love." Compare Eph. 4 : 2.

Ignatius to Polycarp, II, φρόνιμος γίνου ὡς ὁ ὄφις ἐν πᾶσιν καὶ ἀκέραιος εἰσαεὶ ὡς ἡ περιστερά, " Become thou prudent as the serpent in all things, and forever guileless as the dove." Compare Matt. x. 16.

[2] Thus Ignatius, Philad. VII, (τὸ πνεῦμα) οἶδεν γὰρ πόθεν ἔρχεται καὶ ποῦ ὑπάγει, καὶ τὰ κρυπτὰ ἐλέγχει, "It (the Spirit) knoweth whence it cometh and where it goeth, and searcheth out the hidden things." Here John 3 : 8 and 1 Cor. 2 : 10 are blended.

Polycarp to the Philippians, I, ὃν ἤγειρεν ὁ θεὸς λύσας τὰς ὠδῖνας τοῦ ᾅδου · εἰς ὃν οὐκ ἰδόντες πιστεύετε χαρᾷ ἀνεκλαλήτῳ καὶ δεδοξασμένῃ εἰς ἣν πολλοὶ ἐπιθυμοῦσιν εἰσελθεῖν. The quotation from Acts 2 : 24 is inexact, " Whom God raised up, having loosed the pains of Hades." With this are combined a loose quotation from 1 Pet. 1 : 8, "In whom, not having seen, ye believe with joy unspeakable and full of glory"; also an adaptation of 1 Pet. 1 : 12, "into which many desire to enter."

we have μεγαλωσύνης "majesty"; for κρείττων "better,"
μείζων "greater"; and παρ' αὐτοὺς "than they" is
omitted.

Renderings where the sense is given without strict
regard to the text are found frequently in Irenæus,
who is usually careful in quotation. He changes the
syntax, or uses different words intended as equivalents,
as εὐχαρίστησεν for εὐλόγησεν in Luke 2 : 28; ἀκολουθεῖ μοι
for ἔρχεται ὀπίσω μου, in Luke 14 : 27; πεπλανημένον for
ἀπολωλός in Luke 15 : 4. Similarly Origen, Cont. Cels.
8 : 43, gives the equivalent of Eph. 2 : 12 without
exact quotation, τοὺς ξένους τῶν διαθηκῶν τοῦ θεοῦ καὶ
ἀλλοτρίους τῶν εὐαγγελίων.

It is quite possible that a Father may have shaped
a passage to fit his view of a disputed point. Hence,
passages which bear upon great doctrinal controversies
must be examined to see whether they exhibit traces
of intentional alteration in the interest of doctrinal
bias. On the whole, there is little of this. The worst
that can be charged, in the great majority of cases, is
a tendency, where two readings exist, to prefer the one
which makes for the writer's view. Some other cases
may be set down to ignorance of the principles of
textual criticism. Thus Tertullian castigates Marcion
for substituting διαμερισμόν "division" for μάχαιραν
"a sword," in Luke 12 : 51. "Marcion," he says,
"must needs alter, as if a sword could do anything
but divide." But Marcion was right, and Tertullian,
quoting from memory, had in mind the parallel passage in Matt. 10 : 34.[1]

Again, Tertullian stigmatises the Valentinians as
adulterators for reading, in John 1 : 13, οἳ ἐγεννήθησαν,
"which were born." The correct reading, he maintains, is ὃς ἐγεννήθη, "who was born," and the refer-

Influence of dogmatic bias.

[1] Tert. *Adv. Marc.* IV, 2.

ence is to Christ. But the reading of the Valentinians was correct, and Tertullian's reading was absurd, as the context shows.

Similarly, Ambrose charged the Arians with erasing from the text of John 3 : 6, the words, "because the Spirit is God and is born of God," in order to support their denial of the deity of the Holy Ghost. But Ambrose did not know that these words were a gloss which had been incorporated into the western text, and that therefore the Arians were right in omitting it.

Value of patristic quotations in fixing dates of readings.

Patristic quotations have a real value in enabling us to fix, at least approximately, the dates at which certain readings are found. Between A.D. 170 and 250 we have a number of voluminous writers; and in the extant remains of Origen alone the greater part of the New Testament is quoted. On the other hand, the dates of the earliest manuscripts and of some of the versions cannot be fixed with absolute certainty, and the dates of the texts which they contain are still more uncertain. Yet it is to be remembered that, in case of a disagreement between patristic evidence and manuscript authority, the early date of a Father is no guarantee for the value of his evidence, because, contemporary with the earliest Fathers, we have a large amount of textual corruption.

Evidence of patristic quotation to be cautiously used.

It is therefore evident that the testimony of the Fathers to the New Testament text is to be received with great caution, and not without the support of the oldest manuscripts and the versions. Where these agree with patristic testimony, the conclusion is as nearly decisive as it is possible to reach. A striking instance of such agreement appears in the case of the reading in Matt. 19 : 17: τί με ἐρωτᾷς περὶ τοῦ ἀγαθοῦ; "Why dost thou ask me about the good?" as against τί με λέγεις ἀγαθόν; "Why callest thou me good?"

" The critic must be sure (1) that he has the true text of his author before him; (2) what passage it is that the author is quoting (and this is a point about which it is very possible to make mistakes); (3) that the quotation is deliberately taken from a manuscript and not made freely from memory and intended rather as an allusion than a quotation; and (4) what precise reading it was that the manuscript presented. In order to be clear on these points, every single instance of supposed quotation has to be weighed carefully with its context, and only the sifted results of a most extended study can be admitted into the critical apparatus." [1]

The most important sources of this kind of evidence are the writings of Justin Martyr, Tatian, Irenæus, Clement of Alexandria, Hippolytus, Origen, Tertullian, Cyprian, Eusebius, and Jerome.[2]

[1] Sanday, Expositor, 1st Ser., XI, 170.
[2] On Patristic quotations, see G. N. Bonwetsch and H. Achelis, Die christliche griechische Schriftsteller vor Eusebius, *Kirchenväter-Commission der Berliner Academie*, Bd. I, Leipzig, 1897. J. W. Burgon, *The Revision Revised*, London, 1883. Ll. J. M. Bebb, *Evidence of the Early Versions and Patristic Quotations on the Text of the Books of the New Testament*, *Studia Biblica*, II, Oxford. Lists of ancient writers in Tischendorf, *Prolegomena*; Scrivener's *Introduction ;* and E. C. Mitchell, *Critical Handbook of the Greek New Testament*, New York, 1896.

Specific cautions.

PART II

HISTORY OF THE TEXTUAL CRITICISM OF THE NEW TESTAMENT

CHAPTER V

TEXTUAL CRITICISM OF THE EARLY CHURCH

TEXTUAL CRITICISM of the New Testament is a modern science, although attention was very early directed to the condition of the New Testament text.

Corruptions of the text appeared at a very early date. Reuss says, "It may be asserted with tolerable certainty that the farther back we go in the history of the text the more arbitrarily it was treated." Differences between New Testament manuscripts appeared within a century of the time of its composition, and additions and alterations introduced by heretical teachers were early a cause of complaint. Tischendorf says, "I have no doubt that in the very earliest ages after our Holy Scriptures were written, and before the authority of the church protected them, wilful alterations, and especially additions, were made in them." Scrivener says that the worst corruptions to which the New Testament has ever been subjected, originated within a hundred years after it was composed, and Hort agrees with him. Unlike the text of the Koran, which was officially fixed from the first and regarded as sacred, — for a century and a half at least, the greatest freedom

Early appearance of textual corruptions.

42

was exercised in the treatment of the New Testament writings. These writings were not originally regarded as Holy Scripture. Copies of the writings of the Apostles were made for the use of individual communities, and with no thought of placing them on the same level with the Old Testament. Accordingly, there would be little effort at punctilious accuracy, and little scruple in making alterations.

Variants meet us as soon as quotations from the apostolic writings occur at all in later authors, and that both in catholic and heretical writers. Heretics felt the necessity of seeking for their peculiar doctrines a support which should secure for them a place within the church with whose tradition they were, at many points, in conflict. Thus they were driven to interpret the apostolic writings in harmony with their own systems. _{Work of heretics in corrupting the text.}

Accordingly, we find, in the earlier Apologists, allusions to wilful corruptions and misinterpretations. Thus, Irenæus (Adv. Hær. III, 12) declares that "the others (besides Marcion), though they acknowledge the Scriptures, pervert their interpretation." Tertullian (De Præsc. Hær. XXXVIII) says that Marcion and Valentinus change the sense by their exposition. "Marcion," he continues, "has used a sword, not a pen; while Valentinus has both added and taken away." Marcion mutilated the Gospel of Luke in the interest of his antijudaistic views, although it should be said that some of his variations were doubtless taken from manuscripts in circulation in his time. Both Tertullian and Epiphanius go through his work in detail, indicating the mutilation point by point.[1]

---

[1] See J. W. Burgon, *The Revision Revised*, 34, 35. Tertullian, *Adv. Marc.* IV, V. Epiphanius, *Hær.* XLII. Examples of Gnostic interpretations are given by Irenæus (*Adv. Hær.* I, et

Origen's textual comments. Such perversions called forth attempts at textual criticism. Origen (Comm. on Matthew) remarks on the diversity of copies arising either from the negligence of scribes or the presumption of correctors. He frequently discusses various readings, and comments upon the comparative value of manuscripts and the weight of numerical testimony. He seldom attempts to decide on the right reading, being rather inclined to accept all conflicting readings as contributing to edification. His value is in reproducing the characteristic readings which he found. There is no sufficient evidence of a general revision of the text by him, as maintained by Hug.

Manuscripts not carefully prepared. Again, minute care was not exercised in the preparation of manuscripts. In some cases they appear to have issued from a kind of factory, where the work of transcribing was carried on on a large scale. Portions of the same manuscript seem to have been copied from different exemplars and by different hands, and it does not appear to have been thought necessary to compare the two exemplars, or to harmonise the disagreements. Moreover, changes of reading were introduced by individual bishops, who had the sole authority over the public reading of Scripture, and these changes, unless very violent, would soon become as familiar as the old readings, and would pass into the versions.[1]

Reputed revision by Hesychius and Lucian. According to Jerome,[2] Hesychius, an Egyptian bishop, and Lucian, a presbyter and martyr of Antioch, undertook a revision of the New Testament text toward the close of the third century. Our informa-

passim) and by Origen in his commentary on the Fourth Gospel.

[1] See G. Salmon, *Some Criticism of the Text of the New Testament*, 61, 78.

[2] *Adv. Rufinum*, II, 26 ; *De Vir. Ill.* 77 ; *Ad Damasum*.

tion on this work, however, is very meagre. Jerome speaks of it slightingly, and the *Decretum* of Pope Gelasius I, "De libris recipiendis et non recipiendis" (496 A.D.), the genuineness of which, however, is disputed, refers to Hesychius and Lucian as having falsified the Gospels into Apocrypha.[1]

Harmonies of the Gospels, by which are meant constructions of a single continuous narrative out of the four, like that of Tatian, had a tendency to foster alterations made in order to bring the Gospels into harmony of expression as well as of substance.[2]

Of this Jerome complains (Ad Damas.), as also of the transference of marginal glosses to the text. He comments on the number of recensions, which he declares are well-nigh as numerous as the codices, and urges a return to the Greek original, and a correction of those things which have been falsely rendered by vicious interpreters, or perversely emended by presumptuous ignoramuses. In his own revision of the New Testament, begun about 382, Jerome displayed great timidity, and chose codices which did not differ widely from the readings of the Latin.

Jerome complains of alterations of the text.

We repeat, however, that textual criticism is a modern science, and cannot be said to have really existed before the application of printing to the New Testament text. In our discussion of its history it will therefore be more convenient as well as more interesting to combine the history of criticism with that of the printed text.

[1] See B. F. Westcott, *History of the New Testament Canon*, 5th ed., 393, note. O. von Gebhardt, article "Bible Text," in Schaff-Herzog *Encyclopædia*, I, 270. F. J. A. Hort, Westcott and Hort's Greek Testament, Introduction, 181. E. Reuss, *Geschichte der heiligen Schriften des Neuen Testaments*, 5th ed., trans. by Houghton, §§ 367, 368.

[2] See J. Hamlyn Hill, *The Earliest Life of Christ*, etc., 31, 32.

Printing applied earlier to the Old Testament.

Printing was applied to the Old Testament much earlier than to the New. The Jews, by means of their numbers and wealth, were able to command both the skill and the money necessary for the multiplication of the Old Testament in Hebrew, and there was a demand among them for Hebrew books. While no printed edition of the New Testament was made before 1514, the Hebrew Psalter was issued in 1477, and the entire Old Testament in Hebrew in 1488. Portions of the Greek Testament, however, were printed as early as 1486 — the Hymns of Mary and Zacharias — as an appendix to a Greek Psalter, and the first six chapters of the Fourth Gospel appeared in 1504, edited by Aldus Manutius of Venice.

Reasons for delay in printing the New Testament.

The reason for this delay was that the capture of Constantinople by the Turks (1453), and the consequent bondage or exile of the Greek population, were nearly contemporaneous with the invention of printing, thus hindering the efforts of the Greeks to multiply copies of their scriptures. Many of the exiled Greeks earned their living by copying Greek books, and thus had a positive interest in not using the art of printing; and the early attempts at printing Greek were clumsy, so that manuscript was preferred for reading. "So habituated were Greek scholars in that day to read Greek abounding with contractions, many of which were deemed by copyists to be feats of calligraphy, that the endeavours to print Greek with separate types were despised and undervalued" (Tregelles).

The Latin Vulgate reigned supreme and unchallenged in Western Europe, as the only form in which Scripture was known and received. Even theologians had no desire for the original text. The Old Testament in Hebrew was regarded as a book for Jews only. Latin was held to be the only proper medium for the instruction of Christians, and all departures from

Jerome's Version were suspected as dangerous inno-
vations.[1]

The history of the printed text of the New Testa- Periods of
ment and of the accompanying development of textual ment of
criticism falls into three periods: (1) The period of textual
the reign of the Textus Receptus, 1516–1770; (2) The criticism.
transition period from the Textus Receptus to the
older uncial text, 1770–1830; (3) The period of the
dethronement of the Textus Receptus, and the effort
to restore the oldest and purest text by the application
of the genealogical method, 1830 to the present time.

[1] The Latin Vulgate was first published at Mayence in 1455,
in two volumes, known as the Mazarin Bible. The German
Bible was also printed before the Greek and Hebrew original.
At least fourteen editions of the High German Bible were printed
before 1518, and four of the Low German from 1480 to 1522.
See Fritzsche, article "Deutsche Bibelübersetzungen," in Herzog's *Real-Encyklopädie*.

CHAPTER VI

FIRST PERIOD (1516-1770). THE COMPLUTENSIAN
POLYGLOT AND ERASMUS'S GREEK TESTAMENT

ALDUS MANUTIUS, the Venetian publisher, an accomplished scholar, had conceived the plan of a Polyglot of three languages, probably as early as 1497; and in 1501 he submitted a proof-sheet to Conrad Celtes, a German scholar.[1]

Ximenes and the Complutensian. It is, however, to the Spanish cardinal, Ximenes de Cisneros, Archbishop of Toledo, that the honour belongs of preparing the first printed edition of the Greek New Testament.[2]

It was intended to celebrate the birth of the heir to the throne of Castile, afterward Charles V. The cardinal employed for the work the best scholars he could secure, among whom were three converted Jews. The most eminent was James Lopez de Stunica, afterward known for his controversy with Erasmus. The fifth volume of the work, containing the New Testament, was the first completed, in 1514. The printing of the entire work was completed on the 10th of July, 1517. But though the first printed, this was not the first published edition of the Greek Testament. Pope Leo X withheld his approval until 1520, and the work was not issued until 1522, three years after the cardinal's death, and six years after the publication of

First printed but not first published.

[1] The Greek Psalter, in the preface to which the plan is announced, is undated.

[2] For some personal notices of Ximenes, see Scrivener's *Introduction*, II, 176.

PLATE IV

ⷁ

ʰbodie mūʰoīɜ. Ⱌndecī ʳɞ ʳ diſcipuli ʰabie.
rūtˡin ˡgaliłeā ˢin ˡmonte ˣ vbi ᵗconſtituerat
ˢillis ˣieſus. Ⱔˡvidentes ˣeū ʰadorauerūt:
ʰquidā ˡaūᵐdubitauerūt. Ⱔ ʳaccedens
ᵇieſus ˡlocut⁹ ˢeſt ˢeis ˣ dicens. Ⱔata ˢ eſt
ᵐmihi ˡomnis ˢpoteſtas ˢin ˣcelo ˢ et ˢin ꝏ
ˢterra. Ⱔuntes ergo ᵇdocte ˢomnes ꝏꝏ
ᵇgentes: ˡbaptizantes ˢ eos ˢin ᵐnomine ꝏ
ᵐpatris ˢ et ᵖfilij ˢ et ˡſpiritus ˢſancti: ꝏꝏꝏ
ᵇdocentes ˢ eos ˢſeruare ˢomnia ˢ quæcūꝗ̃
ᵇmandaui ˢvobis. Ⱔ ˢecce ˢ ego ˢvobiſcū
ᵇſum ˡomnibus ˢ dieb⁹ ˢvſꝗ̃ ad ᵐᵖſumma=
tionem ˢſeculi.

Ⱔrplicit ᵉuangelium ˢſecundum
ˢⱮattheum.

Ɱaẏ.16.f.
ſup.11.g.
Ⱡuce.10.f.

ˡoṅ ἡμεροῳ.ʳⲟⲩ Ɑⲉ ͛ⲉⲛⲇⲉⲕⲁ ͙ μαθηται ⲉⲡⲟⲣⲉⲩθηⲥⲁⲩ
ͫⲉⲓⲥ ͙ⲧⲏⲩ ͫγⲁⲗⲓⲗⲁⲓⲁⲩ ͫⲉⲓⲥ ͙ⲧⲟ ᵒⲟⲣⲟⲥ ͙ ⲟⲩ ͫⲉⲧⲁⳳⲁⲧⲟ
ᵃⲁⲩⲧⲟⲓⲥ ͙ ⲟ ᵇⲓⲏⲥⲟⲩⲥ ͙ ⲕⲁⲓ ᵈⲓⲇⲟⲛⲧⲉⲥ ͗ⲁⲩⲧⲟⲩ ᵇⲡⲣⲟⲥⲉ
ⲕⲩⲣⲏⲥⲁⲩ ͙ⲁⲩⲧⲟ. ᵈ οⲓ ͙ Ɑⲉ ͫⲉⲇⲓⲥⲧⲁⲥⲁⲩ. ͙ ⲕⲁⲓ ͙ⲡⲣⲟ=
ⲥⲉⲗθⲱⲩ ᵒⲓⲏⲥⲟⲩⲥ ᵉⲉⲗⲁⲗⲏⲥⲉⲩ ᵉⲁⲩⲧⲟⲓⲥ ᵇⲗⲉγⲱⲛ. ᵉ ⲉⲇⲟ̈θⲏ ᵐⲙⲟⲓ ͙ⲡⲁⲥⲁ ᵉⲉⳳⲟⲩⲥⲓⲁ ᵉⲛ ᵉⲟⲩⲣⲁⲛⲱ ͙ ⲕⲁⲓ ᵉⲉⲡⲓ
ᵖγⲏⲥ. ͙ ͫⲡⲟⲣⲉⲩθⲉⲛⲧⲉⲥ ͙ μαθητⲉⲩⲥⲁⲧⲉ ᵖⲡⲁⲛⲧⲁ ͙ⲧⲁ
ᵇⲉθⲛⲏ, ᵇⲁⲡⲧⳳⲟⲛⲧⲉⲥ ͙ⲁⲩⲧⲟⲩⲥ ͙ⲉⲓⲥ ͙ⲧⲟ ᵐⲟⲛⲟμⲁ ͙ⲧⲟⲩ
ᵐⲡⲁⲧⲣⲟⲥ ͙ ⲕⲁⲓ ͙ⲧⲟⲩ ᵖⲩⲓⲟⲩ ͙ ⲕⲁⲓ ͙ⲧⲟⲩ ͙ⲁγⲓⲟⲩ ͙ⲡⲛ̄⁹ ͙
μⲁⲧⲟⲥ: ᵈⲇⲓⲇⲁⲥⲕⲟⲛⲧⲉⲥ ͙ⲁⲩⲧⲟⲩⲥ ᶠⲧⲏⲣⲉⲓⲛ ͙ⲡⲁⲛⲧⲁ ᶠⲟ=
ⲥⲁ ᵉⲉⲛⲉⲧⲉⲓⲗⲁμⲏⲩ ᶠⲩμⲓⲛ. ͙ ⲕⲁⲓ ᵉⲓⲇⲟⲩ ᶠ ⲉγⲱ ᶠ μⲉθ ᵒ ⲩ=
μⲱⲩ ᵇⲉⲓμⲓ ᶠⲡⲁⲥⲁⲥ ͙ⲧⲁⲥ ᵇⲏμⲉⲣⲁⲥ ᵉⲉⲱⲥ ͙ⲧⲏⲥ ᵐⲥⲩⲛⲧⲉ
ⲗⲉⲓⲁⲥ ͙ⲧⲟⲩ ͙ⲁⲓⲱⲛⲟⲥ. ͙ ⲁμⲏⲩ.

Ⱦⲉⲗⲟⲥ ͙ⲧⲟⲩ ᵇⲕⲁⲧⲁ ᵇμⲁⲧθⲁⲓⲟⲩ ᵇⲁγⲓⲟⲩ
ᵇⲉⲩⲁγγⲉⲗⲓⲟⲩ.

Ⱝncipit prologus ſancti Ⱨieronẏmi in euangelium ſecundum Ɱattheum.

Ɱarcus euangeliſta dei electus: et petri in baptiſmate filius:atꝗ̃ in diuino ſermone diſcipulus:ſa
cerdotium in iſrael agens ſecundum carnem leuita:ad fidem chriſti conuerſus:euangeliū in ita
lia ſcripſit oſtendens in eo quid et generi ſuo deberet ⁊ chriſto. Ⱨam initiū̃ principij in voce pro
phetice exclamationis inſtituens:ordinem leuitice electionis oſtendit:vt predicans predeſtinatū
iohānnem filium zacharie in voce angeli annunciatus emiſſum:nō ſolum verbum carnem factum: ſed
et corpus domini in omnia per verbum diuine vocis animatum in initio euangelice predicationis oſtende

(Size of the original page, not including margins, 11 in. × 7¾ in.)

Erasmus's Testament. The entire cost was about $115,000, and only six hundred copies were printed.

This work is known as the Complutensian Polyglot, from Complutum, the Latin name of the town of Alcalà de Henares, the seat of a university, in the district of Guadalajara, a few miles to the northeast of Madrid, where the printing was done. There are six volumes, containing the Old Testament with the Apocrypha, and the New Testament, together with indices, lexica, and other matter. The canonical books of the Old Testament are given in three languages, the Latin Vulgate occupying the place between the Septuagint and the Hebrew. As announced in the Prolegomena, this arrangement signified that Christ (the Roman or Latin Church) was crucified between two robbers (the Jewish Synagogue and the schismatical Greek Church). The New Testament is given in the Greek and in the Latin Vulgate. Its title is: NOVUM TESTA- MENTUM GRÆCE ET LATINE IN ACADEMIA COMPLUTENSI NOUITER IMPRESSUM. Parallel passages and quotations are placed in the Latin margin. The chapters are marked, but not the verses.

The text of the Complutensian was reprinted in several successive editions at Antwerp and Geneva, and also in the Antwerp Polyglot, edited by Spaniards (1571–72), in the great Paris Polyglot (1630–33), and at Mayence in 1753. It was reëdited by Professor P. A. Gratz of Tübingen, along with the Clementine Vulgate, and by Leander Van Ess, with the text of Erasmus incorporated (1827). In Stephen's third edition (see below) it is partially connected with the Textus Receptus. *Reprints of the Complutensian text.*

The important question — What manuscripts were used in the preparation of the New Testament text? — cannot be answered. The editors name but one manuscript (Codex Rhodiensis, Acts), and this has disappeared. They describe their manuscripts generally as *What manuscripts were used?*

E

"antiquissima et emendatissima," and state that they were furnished by Pope Leo X from the Apostolic Library at Rome. But Leo could have sent no New Testament manuscripts, since he was elected less than a year before the New Testament was printed. The library records show that only two manuscripts were sent to Ximenes from the Vatican in Leo's first year, neither of which contained any part of the New Testament.[1] The catalogue of Biblical manuscripts in the library at Alcalà consists exclusively of Hebrew and Latin books, except two containing portions of the LXX. The story that all the New Testament manuscripts at Alcalà were sold as useless parchments to a rocket-maker, in 1749, is without foundation; since all the manuscripts formerly belonging to Ximenes and preserved at Alcalà were transferred to Madrid.

It need not be doubted that the Complutensian editors regarded their manuscripts as ancient and valuable, and intended to use them fairly. The charge of Wetstein and Semler, that they corrupted the text by conforming it to the Latin, is not sustained, which is the more remarkable, in view of the almost idolatrous reverence for the Vulgate indicated in their preface. A few passages, notably 1 John 5:7, 8, afford ground for suspicion, but a careful comparison shows that, in the main, they followed their Greek manuscripts. They were unskilled in criticism, ignorant of the value of manuscripts, and editing the New Testament was a quite new work. There is no evidence that they used B, or any manuscript much resembling it in character, or any other ancient or notably important document. Their text exhibits affinities with certain cursives of

---

[1] Tregelles (*Printed Text*, etc., 7) maintains that the statement of the editors is truthful, and that both Old and New Testament manuscripts were furnished from the Vatican. He makes out a very feeble case.

the eleventh, twelfth, and thirteenth centuries; and, almost invariably, wherever manuscripts of the thirteenth, fourteenth, and fifteenth centuries differ from the most ancient Greek codices and from the quotations of early Greek Fathers, the Complutensian agrees with the modern as against the ancient. The text does not differ widely from that of most codices written from the tenth century downward.[1]

The first published edition of the Greek New Testament was due to the enterprise of a publisher, Froben, the printer of Basle, who, having heard that the Spanish Polyglot was in preparation, resolved to forestall it. Accordingly he secured, in 1515, the services of Desiderius Erasmus, who executed the task of preparing an edition of the Greek Testament with such despatch that the work appeared March 1, 1516, less than six months from the commencement of the printing. Œcolampadius assisted in the correction of the proofs. It was, of course, full of errors, although described in the preface as " diligenter recognitum et emendatum "; and the address to Pope Leo X assured the Pontiff that "non temere neque levi opera, sed adhibitis in consilium compluribus utriusque linguæ codicibus — vetustissimis simul et emendatissimis." Erasmus himself declared, later, that it was "precipitated rather than edited." Dr. Scrivener says, "Erasmus's first edition, in respect of typographical errors, is the most faulty book I know." In order to save time, he even used his manuscripts as printers' "copy."

Character of the Complutensian text.

First published edition.

Erasmus.

---

[1] On the Complutensian Polyglot see Tischendorf, *Prolegomena*, 205 ff. Scrivener, *Introduction*, II, 176 ff. Tregelles, *Printed Text of the Greek Testament.* I. M. Goeze, *Vertheidigung der Complutens. Bibel*, Hamburg, 1765–69. F. Delitzsch, *Studien zur Entstehungsgeschichte der Polyglottenbibel des Cardinal Ximenes*, Leipzig, 1871. C. I. Hefele, *Der Cardinal Ximenes*, 2d ed., Tübingen, 1851.

It formed a large folio of 1027 pages, and contained, along with the Greek text, an elegant Latin version, differing in many respects from the Vulgate. For this version Erasmus had made notes several years before.

Manuscripts employed by Erasmus. Erasmus's first edition was based on a very few manuscripts. Only one of these had any special value (Codex 1, Evang. Act. 1, P. 1, tenth century), and this he almost entirely neglected, indeed, professed to hold it in slight esteem. The basis of his text in the Gospels was an inferior Basle manuscript of the fifteenth century, and in the Acts and Epistles one of the thirteenth or fourteenth century. With these he collated, more or less carefully, one other manuscript of the Gospels, two in the Acts and Catholic Epistles, and three in the Pauline Epistles. None of these was earlier than the tenth century. Of the Apocalypse he had but a single manuscript of the twelfth century, of which Dr. Hort says that with many individualisms and scantily attested readings, it has a large and good ancient element and ought to stand very high among secondary documents (Greek Testament, Introduction, 263). Of

Erasmus's own Greek in the Apocalypse. this manuscript the last six verses were lacking. These Erasmus, who was a better Latinist than Grecian, turned from the Latin into his own Greek. Some portions of this version, which are to be found in no Greek manuscript, still appear in the Textus Receptus.[1]

---

[1] Such are ἀκαθάρτητος for τὰ ἀκάθαρτα τῆς, XVII, 4. The Greek language has no such word as ἀκαθαρτης. Καίπερ ἐστίν for καὶ παρέσται, XVII, 8. Compare Authorized Version, "and yet is." As late as 1883 the first impression of the Revision of Luther's Bible by the German Evangelical Church Conference left this standing; and it was not removed until the last Revision in 1892. Ὀρθρινὸς for πρωϊνός, XXII, 16. Ἐλθέ for ἔρχου, twice, and λαμβανέτω for λαβέτω, XXII, 17. Ἀφαιρῇ for ἀφέλῃ, and ἀφαιρήσει for ἀφελεῖ, XXII, 19. Instances of his use of the Vulgate in order to amend his Greek manuscripts, where he thought them defective, are found in his notes on Acts 9:5,

PLATE V

καλησίαις. ἐγώ εἰμι ἡ ῥίζα, καὶ τὸ γένΘ τοῦ δα
βίδ, ὁ ἀς ὴρ λαμπρὸς, καὶ ὀρθρινὸς. καὶ τὸ πνεῦ
μα καὶ ἡ νύμφη λέγουσιν, ἐλθέ. καὶ ὁ ἀκδωμ--ᷓ--,
ἐιπάτω, ἐλθέ. καὶ ὁ δι τῶψ, ἐλθέτω. καὶ ὁ θέλᷓ--
λοψ, λαμβάνετω τ῀ ὕδωρ ζωῆς, δωρεάψ. συμ
μαρτυροῦμαι γὰρ παν τὶ ἀκούοντι τους λόι
γους προφητείας βιβλίου τ῀τ. ἐ ͂ τις ἐπιθῆ
πρὸς ταῦτα ἐπιθήσει ὁ θεὸς ἐπ᾽ αὐτὸν τὰς πλη/
γὰς τὰς γεγραμμένας ἐν τῶ βιβλίω τ῀τῳ. ͂ ἐ
τις ἀφαιρῇ ἀπ᾽ τ῀ λόγων βίβλε τῆς προφητείας
ταύτης,ἀφαιρήσει ὁ θεὸς τὸ μέρ Θ αὐτο ἀπὸ
βίβλου ζωῆς, καὶ πόλεως ἁγίας, καὶ τῶν γε/
γραμμένων ἐν βιβλίω τούτω. λέγει ὁ μαρτυ
ρῶν ταῦτα. ναὶ· ἔρχομαι ταχύ. ἀμλιι. ναὶ, ἔρι/
χου κύριε ΙΗΣΟΥ. ἡ χάρις τοῦ κυρίου ἡμῶν ΙΗ/
ΣΟΥ ΧΡΙΣΤΟΥ μετὰ πάντωμ ὑμῶμ. ἀμλιι.

cari uobis hæc in ecclesijs. Ego sum ge/
aus & radix Dauid, stella splendida &
matutina. Et spiritus & sponsa dicunt,
ueni.Et qui audit dicat ueni.Et qui sitit
ueniat,& qui uult,accipiat aquam uitæ
gratis. Cõtestor enim omni audienti
uerba pphetiæ libri huius. Si quis ap/
posueri ad hæc,apponet deus super il
lum plagas scriptas in libro isto.Et siqs
diminuerit de uerbis libri pphetiæ hu/
ius,auferet deus partẽ eius de libro ui/
tæ,& de ciuitate sãcta, & de his q̃ scri/
pta sunt in libro isto.Dicit qui testimo
niũ phibet istoꝝ:Etiã,uenio cito.A mẽ.
Etiam Veni dñe Iesu. Gratia dñi no/
stri Iesu Christi cũ oibus uobis. Amen.

Finis Testamenti totius ad græcã ueritatẽ uetustissimorũ Codicum Latinoꝝ
fidem & ad pbatissimoꝝ authorũ citationẽ & interpretationem accu
rate recoguiti, opera studioꝗ D.Erasmi Roterodami.

FACSIMILE OF HALF OF THE LAST PAGE OF ERASMUS'S FIRST EDITION OF
THE GREEK TESTAMENT, SHOWING THE VERSES WHICH ERASMUS REN-
DERED FROM THE VULGATE INTO HIS OWN GREEK

(Size of original page, not including margins, 5¼ in. × 5¼ in.)

Erasmus also refers in his notes to other manuscripts seen by him in his travels, but the allusions are indistinct, and some of the readings are not to be found. That he had heard of B, appears from Sepulveda's correspondence with him in 1533. Sepulveda speaks of a "most ancient Greek exemplar in the Vatican Library, containing both Testaments, most carefully and accurately written in uncial characters, and differing greatly from ordinary copies." [1]

While the work was heartily welcomed in some quarters, it was unsparingly condemned in others. Erasmus's revised Latin Version was regarded as a presumptuous innovation, and many of the theologians of the day were displeased by the annotations in which his alterations were justified. He was attacked by Edward Lee, afterward Archbishop of York, and by Stunica, the Complutensian editor. They complained especially of the omission of 1 John 5:7. Erasmus maintained that it was not an omission, but a non-addition, showing that even some Latin copies did not contain the verse.

Attacks on Erasmus's Testament.

Although the emperor had protected Erasmus's first edition against reprint for four years, it was reproduced by Aldus Manutius, with some variations, but with the most of the typographical errors, at Venice, in 1518. It was placed at the end of the Græca Biblia, the Aldine Septuagint.

Reprinted by Aldus Manutius.

Erasmus himself published four other editions. The second appeared in 1519. He had given much

---

6; 8:37. This manuscript of the Apocalypse was borrowed by Erasmus from Reuchlin, and was retained by Froben, who afterward disposed of it. It lay concealed in the library of the family of Öttingen at Mayhingen, until discovered in 1861 by Fr. Delitzsch. See Delitzsch, *Handschriftliche Funde*, I, 1861–62.

[1] See Scrivener's *Introduction*, I, 109.

Erasmus's later editions. attention in the meantime to examining manuscripts and to revising his own Latin Version; and having besides more leisure, the text of the second edition contained many corrections, both of misprints and readings, the latter mainly on the authority of a fresh codex of the twelfth century. It contains, however, several pages of errors, some of which affected Luther's German Version. Erasmus's revision of his Latin Version called out fresh attacks: for instance, his substitution of " sermo " for " verbum " in John 1:1.[1]

Insertion of 1 John 5:7. The third edition, 1522, differed in several places from the text of the preceding, but was chiefly remarkable for the insertion of 1 John 5:7. The strong feeling excited by its omission from the two former editions had led Erasmus to promise that he would insert it if it could be found in any Greek manuscript. In the interval between 1519 and 1522 there came to hand a manuscript of the sixteenth century, described **Codex Montfortianus.** by Erasmus as Codex Britannicus, but now identified as Codex Montfortianus, at present in the library of Trinity College, Dublin. Its earliest known owner was Froy or Roy, a Franciscan monk, who is believed by some to have written the codex and to have introduced the words from the Vulgate. Erasmus inserted them in the third edition, but, as he wrote in his note, " ne cui sit ansa calumniandi." He continued to regard the passage as spurious.

The fourth edition, 1527, contained the Greek, the Vulgate, and Erasmus's Version, in three parallel columns. Since the publication of the third edition the Complutensian had come into circulation, and Erasmus availed himself of it to make certain corrections, and

---

[1] Dr. Scrivener justly remarks that a minute collation of all Erasmus's editions is greatly to be desired. The number of corrections in the successive editions, as given by Mill, and repeated on Mill's authority by Tregelles, is not reliable.

especially to revise the imperfect text of the Apocalypse, though he did not correct all the readings which
he had himself manufactured by translating from the
Latin. With this exception the fourth edition differed
little from the third. The same was true of the fifth
edition, published in 1535, which, however, omitted the
Vulgate, and retained Erasmus's own Latin Version.[1]

Colinæus. — The edition of Colinæus (Simon de
Colines), Paris, 1534, introduced valuable manuscript
readings, but the edition could not be called critical
The examination of manuscripts was not carried
through. The Erasmian readings in the end of the
Apocalypse were retained. The text, generally speaking, was a mixture of the Erasmian and Complutensian. The edition was not reprinted, and appears to
have had no influence on those which succeeded it.[2]

Colinæus's edition.

[1] See Tregelles, *Printed Text*, 19–29. Scrivener, *Introduction*,
I, 199 f. ; II, 182–187, 401–407. Tischendorf, Prolegomena,
207–211. Fr. Delitzsch, *Handschriftliche Funde*, I, Leipzig,
1861. J. A. Froude, *Life and Letters of Erasmus*. J. Rendel
Harris, *The Origin of the Leicester Codex of the New Testament*,
46–53, London, 1887. O. T. Dobbin, *The Codex Montfortianus*,
etc., London, 1854. E. Reuss, *Bibliotheca Novi Testamenti
Græci*. H. C. Hoskier, *A Full Account and Collation of the
Greek Cursive Codex, Evangelium 604*, Appendix B, the vari-
ous readings by the fifth edition of Erasmus ; Appendix F, re-
port of a visit to the public library at Basle, with facsimile of
Erasmus's second manuscript, Evang. 2, London, 1890. E.
Nestle, *Einführung in das Griechische Neue Testament*, 6–8.
F. J. A. Hort, Greek Testament, Introduction, 103 ff.

[2] Both Reuss and Nestle are disposed to estimate Colinæus's
edition highly. Nestle says that he introduced a series of readings which are generally acknowledged at this day ; and Reuss
gives a list of fifty-two passages in which he stands alone among
early editors. Compare Scrivener, *Introduction*, II, 188. C. R.
Gregory, in Prolegomena to Tischendorf's Testament, says, "In
fifty-two places of those examined by Reuss, Colinæus furnishes
several readings which are to-day approved by many learned
men. "

CHAPTER VII

THE FIRST PERIOD (1516–1770). THE TEXTUS RECEPTUS

Robert
Stephen's
editions.

OF Robert Stephen (Estienne), printer at Paris and protégé of Francis I, it has been said that his biblical work, taken all together, had perhaps more influence than that of any other single man in the sixteenth century. [1] His first two editions, 1546, 1549, were in small 12mo, printed with type cast at the expense of Francis, and issued from the Royal press. They are known as the "O mirificam" editions, from the opening words of the preface, "O mirificam Regis nostri optimi et præstantissimi Principis liberalitatem." In 1550 appeared the third edition, in folio, also from the Royal press, inscribed on the title-page, Βασιλεῖ τ' ἀγαθῷ κρατερῷ τ' αἰχμητῇ, in honour of Henry II, and commonly known as the Editio Regia. Soon after its publication, Stephen, in order to escape from the hounding of the Sorbonne theologians and the censors of the press, removed to Geneva, where he issued his fourth edition, small 12mo, in 1551. The text of the editions of 1546 and 1549 was a compound of the Complutensian and Erasmian texts. [2]

The third (folio) edition, the text of which was

[1] Wordsworth, White, and Sanday, *Old Latin Biblical Texts.*

[2] Scrivener says that his own collation of these two editions gives 139 divergencies in the text and 27 in punctuation, and that in the Apocalypse both editions adhere closely to the Erasmian text, differing from each other in only 11 places.

mainly that of Erasmus's fourth and fifth editions, contained marginal readings from the Complutensian, and from fifteen manuscripts, among which were Codex Bezæ (D), and Codex Parisiensis (Evang. L, eighth century). The collation, both of the Complutensian and of the manuscripts, was partial and slovenly. The text is perpetually at variance with the majority of authorities. Of the Complutensian readings many more were omitted than inserted, and the Complutensian text is often cited incorrectly. The adoption of Erasmus's text causes nearly three hundred departures from the editions of 1546 and 1549.

This, however, was the first collection of various readings of any extent, and, however defective, was of real value to students.[1] *The first collection of various readings.*

The fourth edition, 16mo, contained two Latin Versions, the Vulgate and that of Erasmus, on either side of the Greek text. The text was mainly that of the third edition. Here the division of the text into verses appears for the first time.[2] *First appearance of verse-division.*

---

[1] The manuscripts collated by Stephen have been identified. The two uncials, D and L, are both important. L, of the Four Gospels, is remarkable for its agreement with B, the citations of Origen, and the margin of the Harclean Syriac. Scrivener characterises it as "by far the most remarkable document of its age and class." The cursives are of the tenth, eleventh, twelfth, and thirteenth centuries. No. 10 (Acts, Catholic Epistles, Paul, and Apocalypse, tenth century) has considerable value in the Apocalypse. A list of the manuscripts may be seen in Tischendorf, Prolegomena, 213. Stephen's third edition was republished by Dr. Scrivener, Cambridge, 1859 ; new edition, 1887, and again, 1887, with the variations of the principal editors down to Westcott and Hort and the Revisers.

[2] See Scrivener, *Introduction*, II, 188-192. Tischendorf, Prolegomena, 212 ff. I. H. Hall, on "Chapters and Verses," Schaff-Herzog *Encyclopædia*, I, 433. Also *Journal of the Society of Biblical Literature and Exegesis*, 1883, 1891. Ezra Abbot, "De Versibus," in Tischendorf, Prolegomena, 167-182. H. C.

Beza's editions.

Beza. — Theodore de Bèze, the friend and successor of Calvin in Geneva, and an eminent classical and biblical scholar, besides his own Latin Version in 1556, issued ten editions of the Greek Testament: four in folio, 1565, 1582, 1588, and 1598, and six 8vo, 1565, 1567, 1580, 1591, 1604, 1611. He was not diligent in collecting fresh material for the correction of the text, and he did not make any extensive use of his own D of the Gospels and Acts, and D_2 (Claromontanus) of the Pauline Epistles, sixth century. He was shy of departures from the text of Erasmus and Stephen. His textual basis was Stephen's fourth edition, from which, however, he occasionally diverged, sometimes in favour of the Complutensian, and sometimes of Erasmus, and occasionally substituting new readings. He availed himself of the Oriental Versions, employing Tremellius's Latin Version of the Peshitto, and Franciscus Junius's Latin Translation of the Arabic Version. However, he did not make much use of these. All of his editions vary somewhat from each other, as well as from those of Stephen, yet there is no material difference between any of them. The charge of selecting his readings to suit his theological opinions (Scrivener, II, 193) should be received with caution.

Geneva Bible.

Beza's Latin Translation and Commentary were taken as a guide by the editors of the Genevan Bible, which was originally published in 1560, and with a further revision of the New Testament in fuller harmony with Beza's views, in 1576. The title was, "The New Testament of our Lord Jesus Christ translated out of Greek by Theodore Beza." This work,

Hoskier, *Account and Collation of Codex 604*, etc. ; Appendix B, reprint with corrections of Scrivener's list of differences between Stephen, 1550, and the Complutensian, etc. Tregelles, *Printed Text*, 30 f.

though never formally authorised, exercised the most
marked influence of all the early translations upon the
Authorised Version of 1611, the chief foundations of
which were the editions of 1588 and 1598. It was the
Bible of the household, the most popular in England
up to the advent of King James's Version. It continued to be reprinted until after the middle of the
seventeenth century; many copies were brought to
America by immigrants, and it passed through about
one hundred and sixty editions.[1]

The merit of arranging the Oriental Versions in a
convenient form for Biblical study belongs to the
Antwerp Polyglot, issued in eight volumes folio, **The Ant-**
under the patronage of Philip II, by the publisher, **werp Poly-**
Christopher Plantin, at Antwerp, 1569–72, and **glot.**
edited by the Spanish theologian, Benedict Arias
Montanus. The Greek text appears twice: in Vol. V,
with the Vulgate, the Syrian text and its Latin Translation, and in Vol. VI, with the interlinear version of
Arias. The text is mainly that of the Complutensian,
but agrees in a few places with Stephen, twice with
Erasmus, and once presents a new reading. Thirteen
copies were printed on vellum. The British Museum
has the one prepared for the Duke of Alva.[2]

We now begin to see attention called to the value **Attention**
of patristic quotations in determining the text. Lucas **directed to**
Brugensis, in 1580, prepared annotations on the entire **patristic quotations.**

[1] See Tischendorf, Prolegomena, 214–216. Scrivener, *Introduction*, II, 192 f. J. Eadie, *History of the English Bible*, II,
XXXII–XXXVII. Reuss, *Bibliotheca Novi Testamenti*. Article "Beza," Schaff-Herzog *Encyclopædia*. B. F. Westcott,
History of the English Bible, 296, 297.

[2] See E. Nestle, *Einführung*, etc., 10. Tischendorf, Prolegomena, 215 f. M. Rooses, *Christopher Plantin, Imprimeur An-
versois*, Antwerp, 1884. Id., *Plantin, C. Correspondance*, Gand,
1886. Le Degeorge, *La Maison Plantin à Anvers*, 3d ed., Paris,
1886.

Bible, from Greek and Latin Codices, and from the Syriac Version; and in 1606 edited the four Gospels with a Commentary from Plantin's Polyglot, and with little change of the text. Hugo Grotius, *Polyglotta Londinensia,* freely uses patristic testimony.[1]

The Paris Polyglot. On a still larger scale was the Paris Polyglot of Guy Michel Jay, ten volumes folio. Jean Morin and Gabriel Sionita, a Maronite, were the principal collaborators in preparing the Oriental texts. The two volumes of the New Testament appeared in 1630 and 1633. To the texts of the Antwerp Polyglot it added a Syrian Version of the contested books — 2 Peter, 2 and 3 John, Jude, and the Apocalypse — and an Arabic Version with a Latin rendering. The text was that of the Antwerp Polyglot, with a very few changes.[2]

The Elzevirs. **The Elzevirs and the Textus Receptus.** — The brothers Bonaventure and Abraham Elzevir established a press at Leyden, and issued seven successive editions : 1624, 1633, 1641, 1656, 1662, 1670, 1678. An 8vo edition was printed by them for Whittaker of London, in 1633, with notes by Robert Stephen, Scaliger, Casaubon, and others, and was also issued at Leyden with a new title-page in 1641. The Elzevirs' four later editions were printed in Amsterdam. Their Testaments were very popular because of their small and convenient size and their neat text. The text of the edition of 1624 was drawn chiefly from Beza's 1565, 1582, 1589, and 1598, especially the last, besides Erasmus, the Complutensian and the Vulgate. The second edition (1633) had the verses broken up into separate sentences, instead of having their numbers indicated in the margin as in the edition of 1624. This edition is notable in the history of textual criticism as contain-

---

[1] See Tischendorf, Prolegomena, 216, 221, 1132.

[2] See Tischendorf, Prolegomena, 220. Nestle, *Einführung,* 11.

ing the announcement: "Textum ergo habes nunc AB OMNIBUS RECEPTUM in quo nihil immutatum aut corruptum damus." This is the origin of the familiar phrase Textus Receptus. To this text an almost idolatrous reverence has attached nearly down to the present time. The history of the textual criticism of the New Testament is, largely, the story of gradual emancipation from the tyranny of the Textus Receptus. It has been slavishly followed with slight diversities in hundreds of editions, and substantially represented in all the principal Protestant translations prior to the present century. In some cases attempts to criticise or amend it have been regarded as akin to sacrilege. Yet this sacred text is essentially that of the last edition of Erasmus, framed from a few modern and inferior manuscripts and the Complutensian Polyglot, in the very infancy of Biblical criticism. In more than a score of places it is supported by the authority of no Greek manuscript whatever. The term "Textus Receptus" is, in itself, untruthful. It was put forth simply as a clever advertisement of an enterprising publisher. The edition which bore this pretentious announcement varied somewhat from that of 1624 in the correction of some of the worst misprints, though it retained others equally bad, and added a few of its own.

The term is differently applied in England and on the Continent: in England to Stephen's text of 1550, and on the Continent to the Elzevir of 1633. The differences between these two amount, according to Scrivener, to 287.[1]

(margin note: Textus Receptus. Its influence.)

(margin note: Different applications of the term.)

---

[1] The reverence for the Textus Receptus, and its unhappy effect in retarding the progress of a sound textual criticism, may be seen in Dean J. W. Burgon's *Revision Revised*, London, 1883, in the works of Dr. Scrivener, and in the views of the Rev. E. Miller, in the *Oxford Debate on the Textual Criti-*

Textus
Receptus
repudiated
by modern
scholarship.

The best textual scholarship of the present day re-pudiates the Textus Receptus as a textual basis. The latest and best Concordance to the New Testament (Moulton and Geden, 1897) entirely ignores its read-ings.[1]

cism of the New Testament, London, 1897. *The Expositor's Greek Testament* (I, 1897), edited by W. Robertson Nicoll, and professing to give the latest results of critical scholarship, adopts the Receptus as its textual basis. It has been the policy of the British and Foreign Bible Society to circulate in Germany only reprints of the Textus Receptus. As late as 1893–94 that society printed at Cologne over twelve thousand copies of this text, and went on to circulate, in Germany and Switzerland, about six-teen hundred copies per annum. In order to counteract this, the Württemburgian Bible Society at Stuttgart published last year a Greek Testament with a critically revised text, based on a col-lation of the editions of Tischendorf, Westcott and Hort, Wey-mouth, and Bernhard Weiss, adding for the Gospels and Acts a selection of manuscript readings, chiefly from Codex Bezæ. It is an admirable specimen of typography, and can be purchased for about twenty-five cents.

[1] See Tischendorf, Prolegomena, 216 ff. Scrivener, *Introduc-tion*, II, 193–195. A. Willems, *Les Elzevier: Histoire et Annales Typographiques*, Bruxelles et Paris, 1880. F. H. A. Scrivener, *The New Testament in the Original Greek according to the Text followed in the Authorised Version, together with the Variations adopted in the Revised Version*, Cambridge, 1881. He gives a list of the passages in which the Authorised Version departs from the readings of Beza, 1598. H. C. Hoskier, *A Full Account and Collation of the Greek Cursive Codex Evang. 604.* Appendix C, a full and exact comparison of the Elzevir editions of 1624 and 1633.

CHAPTER VIII

THE FIRST PERIOD (1516–1770). THE BEGINNINGS OF A CRITICAL METHOD

WE have now reached the point where the preparation for effective criticism begins. Up to this time the
work had been chiefly the collection and registering of
evidence. Manuscripts were collated, and their various readings noted, but no comparison of them was
attempted. In the earlier editions the evidence was
scanty in amount and inferior in quality. The principal uncials were either unknown or inaccessible.
Neither D or D$_2$ were much used by Beza, who held
closely by the texts of Erasmus and Stephen. The
Oriental Versions had been printed in the Antwerp
Polyglot, but were used by Beza only to a limited extent and through Latin translations. Lucas Brugensis and Grotius had only broken ground in the matter
of patristic citations. The text of the Vulgate was
faulty, and revisions like those of Erasmus and Beza
were suspected and frowned upon by the ecclesiastical
authorities. The body of manuscript evidence amassed
by the Stephens was imperfectly collated in the edition of 1550. Though the authorities stand in the
margin, the text is perpetually at variance with the
majority of them, and, in 119 places, with all of them.
No fixed principles regulated the occasional applications of the manuscript readings to the construction of
the text. Neither the true value of various readings

63

nor the necessity for accuracy in collation was appreciated or understood. With the occasional adoption of fresh manuscript readings, mostly of a common and late type, the text remained substantially Erasmian, with some modifications from the Complutensian, except in those editions which had a Complutensian basis. The crystallisation into a fixed and received text which followed was due mostly to the beauty of the Stephen and Elzevir editions, and to the pretentious and groundless advertisement of the Leyden printers. The Textus Receptus perpetuated some of the grossest errors of Erasmus.

Codex A brought to England.

The impulse to a new development of textual science was given in England, about the middle of the seventeenth century, through the gift, in 1628, of the Alexandrian manuscript to Charles I, by Cyril Lucar, the Patriarch of Constantinople. France contributed a powerful auxiliary in Richard Simon, whose writings had a large share in undermining the general acquiescence in the Received Text.[1]

Richard Simon.

Walton's Polyglot.

Walton's Polyglot. — In England the way was led by Brian Walton, afterward Bishop of Chester, with his *London Polyglot*, issued in 1657 in six volumes folio. The fifth volume, containing the New Testament, gives Stephen's text of 1550, with the readings of A at the foot. This notation marks the origin of the practice of designating the uncials by capitals. The sixth volume is devoted to a critical apparatus gathered from a number of authorities, including D, D₂,

---

[1] Simon's principal works on the New Testament were: *Histoire Critique du Texte du Nouveau Testament*, Rotterdam, 1689; *Histoire Critique des Principaux Commentateurs du Nouveau Testament . . . avec une Dissertation Critique sur les Principaux Actes Manuscrits*, Rotterdam, 1693. Reuss says that Simon surpassed all his predecessors and his successors for a long time after, in point of sound historical learning, acumen, and comprehensive grasp of the materials.

PLATE VI

FACSIMILE OF EXTRACTS FROM A PAGE OF WALTON'S POLYGLOT, SHOWING THE VERSIONS OF PAUL'S EPISTLE TO THE ROMANS, CHAPTER I, IN LATIN, GREEK, SYRIAC, and ETHIOPIC, ON THE SAME PAGE

(Size of original page, from which one-half has been reproduced, 15 7/8 in. × 9¼ in., not including margins.)

and the copies in Stephen's margin. The most of these authorities had never been used before. Of the manuscripts, which include the famous Codex Montfortianus (see under Erasmus), three are of the fifteenth century, one of the fifteenth or sixteenth, three of the twelfth, and one of the twelfth or thirteenth. Two, Evang. 59 and Act. 36, are valuable. Walton also gave the Velesian and Wechelian readings, which were of no value.[1] Besides the Greek text, the Polyglot contained the Latin Vulgate, the Peshitto, Ethiopic and Arabic Versions, besides a Persian Version of the Gospels, and the later Syriac of the five books not contained in the Peshitto (2 Peter, 2 and 3 John, Jude, Apocalypse). Each Oriental Version was accompanied by a collateral Latin translation.[2] Walton's work thus consisted in adding to the materials of criticism. The versions in the fifth volume furnish a valuable store of material. He is charged, however, with suppressing

Manuscripts used by Walton.

[1] The Velesian readings were a collection written in vermilion in the margin of a copy of Stephen's Editio Regia by Faxardo, Marquis of Velez, a Spaniard, who was said to have taken them from sixteen manuscripts, eight of which were in the Escorial. They were afterward shown to have been collected by Velez from Latin manuscripts.

The Wechelian readings were from the margin of a Bible printed at Frankfurt, 1597, by the heirs of Andrew Wechel. All of these readings are found in Stephen's margin, or in the early editions.

[2] Walton was a Royalist during the Civil War, and was chaplain to Charles I; but the Polyglot was published under the patronage of Cromwell, who allowed the paper to be imported free of duty. After the Restoration, Walton, appointed Bishop of Chester by Charles, issued a new preface, in which Cromwell was styled "maximus ille draco." Accordingly there are two kinds of copies, — *the Republican*, with compliments to Cromwell in the preface, but with no dedication, and *the Loyal*, dedicated to Charles II. This was the first work published by subscription in England.

F

a large part of the collations which had been sent to him.[1]

Curcellæus. — One year after the publication of Walton's Polyglot, appeared the Greek Testament of Stephen Curcellæus, or Courcelles, with a learned introduction, parallel texts, and many various readings, some from two or three fresh manuscripts. He repeated the Elzevir text of 1633, with a few changes, enclosing 1 John 5:7 in brackets. He did not, however, give the authorities for his readings, and those drawn from manuscripts were mingled with conjectures of his own. As these conjectures were manifestly shaped by Socinian views, his Testament tended to discourage critical study as something aimed at the integrity and authority of Scripture. Its appearance so soon after Walton's Polyglot reacted unfavourably upon the latter, and created alarm at the collection of readings presented by Walton. The principal merit of Curcellæus's Testament consists in his collection of parallel texts. In his preface he gives an account of the earlier editions, and asserts that it is not yet time to judge of readings, but to collect and preserve them; and that the suppression of them is the real source of the increasing corruption.[2]

Curcellæus's Testament. Reacts unfavourably upon Walton's Polyglot.

---

[1] See Tischendorf, Prolegomena, 220. Scrivener, *Introduction*, II, 197 ff. J. Rendel Harris, *Origin of the Leicester Codex of the New Testament*, London, 1887. Henry Stevens, *The Bibles in the Caxton Exhibition*, London, 1877. John Owen, *Of the Integrity and Purity of the Hebrew Text of the Scriptures, with Considerations on the Prolegomena and Appendix to the late Biblia Polyglotta*, Oxford, 1659. B. Walton, *The Considerator Considered*, London, 1659. S. P. Tregelles, *Printed Text*, etc., 38. H. J. Todd, *Memoirs of the Life and Writings of Brian Walton, together with the Bishop's Vindication of the London Polyglot Bible*, London, 1821. E. Reuss, article "Polyglottenbibeln" in Herzog's *Real-Encyklopädie*.

[2] See Tischendorf, Prolegomena, 222. Scrivener, *Introduction*, II, 198. Tregelles, *Printed Text*, 39.

Fell. — It was with a view to counteract the unfavour- able impression created by Walton and Curcellæus, that John Fell, Dean of Christ Church, and subsequently Bishop of Oxford, issued his Greek Testament at Oxford in 1675. It was of small size, with the various readings at the foot of the pages, along with the authorities by which they were supported. The title-page announced that the text was drawn from more than a hundred manuscripts. The margin contained citations from the Memphitic and Gothic Versions. He gave the readings of a very few manuscripts not previously collated, and added in his appendix the Barberini collection of readings.[1]

Fell's text was mainly that of the Elzevir of 1633. Little attention was given to patristic testimony.[2]

Mill. — Walton, Curcellæus, and Fell, particularly the last, prepared the way for John Mill, whose edition of the Greek Testament, published in folio, Oxford, 1707, marked the foundation of textual criticism. His preparations for the work were begun about 1677, and were encouraged and promoted by Fell, and later by the patronage of Queen Anne. His merit was largely that of a collector of critical material. He gave much attention to patristic testimony, and also to the Vul-

[1] This was a collection made by John Matthew Caryophilus of Crete, about 1625, with a view to an edition of the Greek Testament. It is described as " Collationes Græci contextus omnium librorum Novi Testamenti juxta editionem Antverpiensem regiam cum XXII codicibus antiquis MSS." This was edited by Peter Poussin in 1673, and was found in the Barberini Library at Rome, in 1785, by Andrew Birch, along with the petition of Caryophilus to Pope Paul V for the loan of six manuscripts in the Vatican. These included B, and S (tenth century), which is among the earliest dated manuscripts of the Greek Testament. The Barberini readings often favour the Latin Version, and have been superseded.

[2] See Tischendorf, Prolegomena, 222. Scrivener, *Introduction*, II, 199 f. Tregelles, *Printed Text*, 40.

gate and Itala. His knowledge of Oriental languages was limited, so that he was obliged to depend mainly on the Latin translations in Walton's Polyglot.

As a collator, he was not accurate according to the modern standard of textual scholarship. He collected rather than classified manuscripts, although he frequently records his judgment of the value of readings, and exhibits a foreshadowing of the genealogical method in noting relationships between manuscripts, and between manuscripts and particular versions. The catalogue of his manuscripts may be seen in Tischendorf, Prolegomena, 226. He made no attempt to construct a new text, but used that of Stephen's 3d ed., varying from it in a few places. His Prolegomena consisted of three parts: (1) The canon of the New Testament. (2) The history of the text, including quotations of the Fathers and early editions. (3) The plan and contents of his own work. Of the Prolegomena Dr. Scrivener says, "Though by this time too far behind the present state of knowledge to bear reprinting, they comprise a monument of learning such as the world has seldom seen, and contain much information the student will not even now easily find elsewhere." His New Testament was republished in folio, in 1710, at Amsterdam and Rotterdam, by Ludolph Kuster, who arranged in its proper places the matter which Mill had put into his appendix, because he had received it too late for incorporation into his critical notes. He added the readings of twelve fresh manuscripts. He was the first to give a definite statement of the number of various readings in the New Testament text, estimating them at thirty thousand, a number which appears trifling in the light of later critical results.[1]

Fore-shadows the genealogical method.

First estimate as to number of variations.

---

[1] Mill's Testament was attacked by Dr. Whitby in 1710. The details of the controversy may be read in Tregelles's *Printed*

Gerhard von Maestricht, Toinard, Wells. — The year after the appearance of Kuster's *Mill*, Gerhard von Maestricht published at Amsterdam a New Testament in 8vo, containing all the critical matter of Fell's edition, a collation of one Vienna manuscript, forty-three canons for the examination of various readings and discussions upon them, with other matter, especially parallel texts. The text is Fell's. A second improved edition was issued in 1735. This appears to have been the first attempt to lay down canons for various readings.[1]

The *Evangeliorum Harmonia Græco-Latina* of Nicholas Toinard, of Orleans, was published in the same year as Mill's New Testament. Toinard was the first Roman Catholic since Erasmus, and the last before Scholtz (1830), who undertook a critical edition. In his Prolegomena he announces that he has made a Greek Testament according to the two oldest Vatican codices and the Old Latin Version, where it agreed with them. He was thus working on the same principle afterward proposed by Bentley.[2]

Edward Wells put forth an edition, 1709–19, in ten parts, containing a Greek text, an English version and paraphrase, critical and exegetical notes, and historical dissertations. More boldly than his predecessors, he introduced new manuscript readings into the text. His text was marked by frequent departures

Text. It called out Richard Bentley's celebrated monograph, *Remarks upon a Discourse of Free-thinking, by Phileleutherus Lipsiensis.* See Tischendorf, Prolegomena, 224–227. Scrivener, *Introduction*, II, 200. Tregelles, *Printed Text*, 41–49. Hort, Westcott and Hort's *New Testament*, Introduction, 180. J. H. Monk, *Life of Richard Bentley, D.D.*, London, 1833.

[1] See Tischendorf, Prolegomena, 229. Scrivener, *Introduction*, II, 204.

[2] See Tischendorf, Prolegomena, 227 f. Reuss characterises the *Harmonia* as "liber rarissimus."

from the Elzevir, and his agreement with later critics, as Griesbach, Lachmann, and Tischendorf, is noteworthy.[1]

It will be noticed that in Toinard and Wells there appear signs of restlessness under the pressure of the Textus Receptus, a growing tendency to emphasise manuscript authority, and attempts at a reconstruction of the text; while in Gerhard von Maestricht, as in Mill, we see signs of a movement toward the classification of documents.

Bentley's Proposals.

Bentley. — This "glimpse of the genealogical method," which was the most important contribution to the criticism of the period between Mill and Lachmann, received a more definite development in the *Proposals* of Richard Bentley, Master of Trinity College, Cambridge. In 1691 he had urged Mill to publish in parallel columns the Greek text of A and the Græco-Latin texts of D, D_2, and E_2. In 1720 he issued his *Proposals* for printing an edition of the Greek New Testament and the New Testament of the Vulgate Version, " per Stum. Hieronymum ad vetusta exemplaria Græca castigatæ et exactæ," both from the most ancient codices, Greek and Latin. The *Proposals* closed with the last chapter of the Apocalypse in Greek and Latin as a specimen.

Bentley's hypothesis.

Bentley's hypothesis was, that the oldest manuscripts of the Greek original and of Jerome's Vulgate resemble each other so closely that, by means of this agreement, he could restore the text as it stood in the fourth century, so that there should not be a difference of twenty words, or even particles. "By taking two thousand errors out of the Pope's Vulgate (the Clementine), and as many out of the Protestant Pope Stephen (ed. of 1550), I can set out an edition of each in columns, without using any book under nine hundred

---

[1] See Tischendorf, Prolegomena, 228.

years old, that shall so exactly agree, word for word, and order for order, that no two tallies nor two indentures can agree better." In order to confirm the readings introduced into the text, he proposed to make use of the Syriac, Coptic, Gothic, and Ethiopic Versions, and of all the Greek and Latin Fathers within the first five centuries, and to exhibit all the various readings within those five centuries.

For the prosecution of this design it was necessary that the manuscripts of the Vulgate should be collated as carefully as those of the Greek Testament; and much work both in collection and collation was done by Bentley himself, and by his colleague, John Walker, in Paris, by Chevalier in Tours, and Casley in Oxford. Their collations are preserved in the Library of Trinity College, Cambridge.[1] They are more on the Latin Vulgate than on the original Greek. The most valuable of the collations, that of B, was procured about 1720, at Bentley's expense, and by the labour of the Abbate Mico, and was revised by Abbate Rulotta in 1729. *Collections and collations for Bentley's work.*

These collations are all that remain of Bentley's enterprise, for the work itself never appeared. Yet the *Proposals* mark an important step in the history of textual criticism. They indicate an advance toward discrimination in the selection and use of Greek manuscripts, and a frank and vigorous protest against the tyranny of the Textus Receptus. Bentley was the first to lay down the great principle that the whole text is to be formed on evidence, apart from the influence of any edition. He declared that after the Complutenses and Erasmus, who had but very ordinary manuscripts, the New Testament became the property of booksellers, and that Stephen's text stood as if an apostle was his compositor. He described *Importance of the Proposals.*

---

[1] See Catalogue in Scrivener's *Introduction*, II, 89 f.

Stephen as the Protestant Pope. Of the text of the
Vulgate he asserted that Popes Sixtus and Clement
were incompetent to execute its revision, since they
were mere theologians, without experience in manuscripts, using inferior Greek copies, and mistaking
later copies for earlier. He perceived the division-line
between the old and the late codices, and insisted that
the ancient manuscripts are the witnesses of the ancient text. He was even prepared to dismiss from consideration the testimony of the whole mass of modern
copies.

"The New Testament," wrote Bentley, "has been
under a hard fate since the invention of printing.

"After the Complutenses and Erasmus, who had but
very ordinary manuscripts, it became the property of
booksellers. . . . . No heathen author has had such
ill fortune. Terence, Ovid, etc., for the first century
after printing, went about with twenty thousand errors
in them. But when learned men undertook them, and
from the oldest manuscripts set out correct editions,
those errors fell and vanished. But if they had kept
to the first published text, and set the various lec-
tions only in the margin, those classic authors would
be as clogged with variations as Dr. Mill's Testament is.

"Popes Sixtus and Clement, at a vast expense, had
an assembly of learned divines to recense and adjust
the Latin Vulgate, and then enacted their new edition
authentic; but I find, though I have not discovered
anything done *dolo malo*, they were quite unequal to
the affair. They were mere *theologi*, and had no experience in manuscripts, nor made good use of Greek
copies, and followed books of five hundred years before
those of double age. Nay, I believe they took these
new ones for the older of the two; for it is not everybody knows the age of a manuscript."

Bentley's proposals were comprised in eight paragraphs : the first spoke of the actual condition of the printed Greek Testament and the Latin Vulgate, and the importance of the service of revising both, on the authority of manuscripts of more than a thousand years old. The second related to the view which Bentley took of certain passages in St. Jerome "where he declares, that (without making a new version) he adjusted and reformed the whole Latin Vulgate to the best Greek exemplars, that is to say, to those of the famous Origen," and also of the passage containing Jerome's statement that the *order* even of the words is important in translations of Holy Scripture. From these passages he concluded that the oldest Greek and Latin copies ought to agree both in words and in their order, "and upon making the essay (he says) he has succeeded in his conjecture beyond his expectation or even his hopes." In the third paragraph he states his belief that the mass of various readings may, from his collations, be so reduced in number as to leave only about two hundred places in which the true text of a passage can be a matter of doubt. In the fourth, he says that he uses as subsidiary, in order to confirm the readings which he adopts, "all the old versions, Syriac, Coptic, Gothic, and Ethiopic, and all the Fathers, Greeks and Latins, within the first five centuries "; and he gives in his notes all the various readings (now known) within the said five centuries. So that the reader has under one view what the first ages of the church knew of the text; and what has crept into any copies since is of no value or authority. In the fifth paragraph, Bentley disclaims the use of conjecture altogether in the text itself of the sacred volume; the notes are to contain all the evidence on which every word rests; and also the common readings of Stephen's Greek and Clement the VIIIth's Latin are to be plainly exhibited.

In the sixth, the reader is told that any conjectures of the editor will be given, as such, in the Prolegomena, in which, also, there was promised a full account of the manuscripts, etc., used. The seventh paragraph informed the reader of the terms of subscription, three guineas for smaller paper, five for large. The concluding paragraph promised that the edition should be put to press as soon as a sufficient sum was subscribed.

Conyers Middleton attacks the *Proposals*. Bentley's proposals were attacked in an anonymous pamphlet by Conyers Middleton, which was severely replied to in another anonymous pamphlet, commonly attributed to Bentley. Middleton rejoined in a longer and abler pamphlet; but he was no match for Bentley, and his reply did not bear upon the critical points at issue. An unhappy consequence of the controversy was the impression that criticism could not be safely applied to the text of the New Testament, and that it is better to retain traditional readings without evidence than to revise them according to competent testimony.

Had Bentley's edition appeared, it would have presented an invaluable body of critical materials. It would have been an important contribution to the establishment of a settled text, and a severe blow at the traditional Textus Receptus. His text would have been that of the Greek manuscripts which resemble the oldest copies of the Vulgate; but this would have been only the text current in the West, and not that of the whole body of Christian readers in the third and fourth centuries.

Bentley's faith in his hypothesis weakened. But this hypothesis of substantial identity between the oldest Greek and Latin copies was more favoured by A than by any other really ancient document. The impossibility of settling the text by the application of this principle appears to have grown upon him, especially after his acquaintance with the Vatican readings; and it is to this that some impute the abandonment of his project.[1]

Mace. — The revolt against the Textus Receptus was continued by William (or Daniel) Mace, a Fellow of Gresham College, London, who published anonymously, in 1729, a Greek and English Diglott, with the title *The New Testament in Greek and English, containing the Original Text corrected from the Authority of the Most Authentic Manuscripts*, etc. His emendations agree remarkably with readings approved by critics of this day. Reuss speaks of him as one whom his contemporaries unjustly persecuted, and whom more recent critics much more unjustly consign to oblivion.[2]

Mace anticipates readings of modern critics.

[1] See Tregelles, *Printed Text*, 57–68. Tischendorf, Prolegomena, 231. Wordsworth, White, and Sanday, *Old Latin Biblical Texts*, I, XXV. J. H. Monk, *Life of Richard Bentley, D.D. The Works of Richard Bentley, D.D.*, collected and edited by A. Dyce, London, 1836. *Bentlei et Doctorum Virorum ad eum Epistolæ*, 2d ed., Leipzig, 1825.

[2] As Scrivener, *Introduction*, II, 210, "The anonymous text and version of William Mace, said to have been a Presbyterian minister, are alike unworthy of serious notice, and have long since been forgotten." These words, in which Dr. Scrivener apparently echoes Tregelles (*Printed Text*, 65), are in marked contrast with the remarks of Dr. C. R. Gregory, in his Prolegomena to Tischendorf's 8th ed., 240. Nestle also alludes to him as perhaps the boldest deviator from the Received Text (*Einführung*, 15).

CHAPTER IX

THE FIRST PERIOD (1516-1770). MOVEMENT TOWARD THE GENEALOGICAL METHOD

Recognition of the relationship of documents.

TEXTUAL CRITICISM now began to feel its way toward a new method, through the growing recognition of the relationship of documents, foreshadowed by Mill and Bentley. This led up to the classification of all documents by families — a principle which was first clearly announced by Bengel in 1734. This principle shapes the whole subsequent development of New Testament textual criticism. In order that the remaining stages of the history may be understood, it will be necessary to anticipate certain features of later criticism.

Statement of certain features of later criticism necessary for understanding the remaining history.

It may be well to remind the reader once more that the problem of Textual Criticism is to extract from all attainable sources, as nearly as possible, the original text of the author; and that this process involves the comparison of thousands of various readings, and the selection of those which represent the purest text.

No sound decision as to the comparative value of readings can be reached by a merely numerical process, that is to say, by giving preference to that reading which is contained in the majority of manuscripts; for it cannot be asserted that a reading has the majority of witnesses, until all known manuscripts have been collated, and all unknown manuscripts have been discovered and collated. There may be enough manuscripts unknown and uncollated to turn the scale in favour of a rejected reading. Moreover, this process

76

takes account only of the number, and not at all of the quality, of the witnesses. The united value of the readings of ten manuscripts may not equal that of four others. The ten may all be of late date and inferior quality, while the four may include two or three of the earliest and best.

Thus the clause ἀλλὰ ῥῦσαι ἡμᾶς ἀπὸ τοῦ πονηροῦ, "deliver us from the evil one," which is attested by every known authority in Matt. 6 : 13, is omitted by the highest textual authorities from Luke xi. 4. Yet the evidence in its favour, numerically considered, is very strong. It is found in ACDEFGHKMRSUVΓΔΛΠ, in a number of cursives, in the Old Latin *b c f ff i l q*, and in the Bohairic, Peshitto, Curetonian and Harclean Syriac, and the Ethiopic Versions. But it is wanting in ℵ and B. B does not contain it at all, and ℵ only by a hand three centuries later than the first. Again, in Mark 7 : 19, eight later uncials and hundreds of cursives have the Received reading καθαρίζον πάντα τὰ βρώματα, "purging all meats," the neuter participle "purging" agreeing with the clause "goeth forth into the draught." On the other hand, ℵABEFGHLSXΔ and three Fathers have καθαρίζων, the masculine participle, referring to Christ, "This he said, making all meats clean." The *numerical* superiority is with the former reading; the *weight*, both of authority and sense, is with the latter.

Neither can a sound conclusion be reached on the basis of the comparative age of manuscripts. The important point is the age of the text contained in the manuscript relatively to the autograph. A manuscript of the fourth century may have been copied from one only a little older than itself, and that in turn from one only a little older; while a manuscript of the eleventh century may have been copied from one of the third century, and that from the autograph.

An ancient text not necessarily a pure text.

But an ancient text is not necessarily a pure text. Some of the worst textual corruptions had entered in the second century. Therefore the readings must be scrutinised in order to discover what evidence they afford of their own purity. To this process two kinds of evidence are applied, Intrinsic and Transcriptional.

Intrinsic and Transcriptional evidence.

By Intrinsic evidence is meant that which is furnished by knowledge of the writer's style and habits of thought; by grammatical considerations, the nature of the context, etc. This kind of evidence goes to show which of several readings of a passage is most likely to have proceeded from the writer's own hand. By Transcriptional evidence is meant that which is derived from knowledge of the habits of scribes, and of the accidents to which they are liable in the process of transcription. This class of evidence goes to show which one of several readings the copyist is likely to have had before him, and which one is most likely to have been changed into the several various readings.

Caution in the use of intrinsic probability.

In the matter of intrinsic probability it is easy to make a mistake. Conclusions founded upon it are to be accepted with great caution, because of the tendency of the critic to form his conclusion from his own point of view or his own environment, rather than from those of the author. Thus, intrinsic probability seems to point to the omission of the words, "Make me as one of thy hired servants," from Luke 15 : 21, repeating the words of ver. 19. From our point of view it seems unlikely that the restored son, with the full assurance of pardon, would repeat the request which he had proposed to himself before his experience of the riches of fatherly love and forgiveness. A large number of manuscripts and most of the versions omit the words. Westcott and Hort bracket them; Tischendorf rejects them. Yet we cannot rest solely on intrinsic probability from our point of view.

The words are attested by ℵ B D U X. Similarly, a critic may light on an ungrammatical reading and be tempted to emend on the ground of the intrinsic improbability of the writer's grammatical blunder; yet a larger acquaintance with his habits of composition may greatly diminish that improbability. So of awkwardness of style, or inconsistency. Because Phil. 1:22 presents a very awkward construction, because Rom. 5:12 introduces us to a puzzling parenthetical passage, it cannot be certainly inferred that Paul originally wrote these in a less awkward form, and that corruptions have crept into the text, for Paul's writings are full of such instances.

There are rare instances in which intrinsic probability may carry the day even against strong manuscript evidence. In Mark 6:22, ℵ B D L Δ give ἀσελθούσης τῆς θυγατρὸς αὐτοῦ Ἡρωδιάδος καὶ ὀρχησαμένης, "*His* daughter Herodias having entered in and danced." This reading appears in the text of Westcott and Hort. Yet, in the face of such manuscript evidence, it is safe to say that Mark could not have intended this. The statement directly contradicts Josephus, who says that the name of the damsel was Salome, and that she was the daughter of Herod Philip, by Herodias, who did not leave her husband until after Salome's birth. It is, moreover, most improbable that even Herod the Tetrarch would have allowed his own daughter thus to degrade herself.

Intrinsic probability occasionally prevails against manuscript evidence.

Conclusions as to transcriptional probability are somewhat more reliable because of our knowledge of the habits of scribes. We can detect with some accuracy motives for intentional alteration and reasons for unintentional errors. It is easy to understand how a scribe might think himself in duty bound to play the part of a corrector, and conform an unfamiliar inflexion or quotation or construction to forms familiar

Transcriptional probability more reliable.

to himself. He might think it incumbent on him to change ἤλθατε, ἤλθαν, into ἤλθετε, ἤλθον; or to alter λήμψομαι and προσωπολημψία into λήψομαι and προσωποληψία for the sake of euphony; or to write ἡμέρας instead of ἡμέραι in Matt. 15:32, on the ground that correct grammar required the accusative of duration. Or, again, he might substitute κράξαν and σπαράξαν for κράξας and σπαράξας in Matt. 9:26, in order to make the participles agree with the neuter πνεῦμα. The correct reading in Mark 1:2 is ἐν τῷ Ἡσαΐᾳ τῷ προφήτῃ, "in Isaiah the prophet;" but it is apparent that some scribe found it difficult or impossible to account for the fact that the quotation from Isa. 40:3, "The voice of one crying," etc., is preceded by a quotation from Mal. 3:1, "Behold I send my messenger," etc.; and accordingly substituted ἐν τοῖς προφήταις, "in the prophets."

Intentional alterations from the desire to amplify.   Intentional alterations may also have proceeded from the desire to amplify. It is well known that copyists were in the habit of making a quoted passage, for instance, as full as possible, through fear of losing something which the writer had said. For example, Matt. 15:8. The Received Text is ἐγγίζει μοι ὁ λαὸς οὗτος τῷ στόματι αὐτῶν, καὶ τοῖς χείλεσί με τιμᾷ, "This people draweth nigh unto me with their mouth and honoureth me with their lips." The best modern texts read ὁ λαὸς οὗτος τοῖς χείλεσί με τιμᾷ, "This people honoureth me with their lips." At least fourteen uncials support the longer reading, yet the weight of authority is in favour of the shorter: ℵ B D L T, Vulgate, Curetonian, Armenian, Æthiopic, Origen, Chrysostom. The Received Text is most probably an amplification of the shorter and genuine reading.

Insertions of readings of one Gospel in another.   It is also well known how habitually copyists inserted in one Gospel the readings of another, so as to bring them into agreement. There is not a manuscript or a version that has not suffered more or less in this manner.

As for unintentional errors, there are many ways in which they have slipped into the text; as by confounding letters of similar appearance, omitting an entire verse when two successive lines or sentences end with the same word, and the scribe has mistaken the second ending for that which he has just written; misreadings of abbreviations; adopting marginal glosses into the text, etc. See Chapter II. Such knowledge of the habits of scribes may help us greatly in determining what reading the copyist is likely to have had before him, and which of several readings is most likely to have been changed into another or several others. In any case in which intrinsic and transcriptional probability concur, the concurrence makes in favour of the reading. In Phil. 1 : 7, for example, ℵ B Dᵇᶜ E K L P repeat ἐν. In A D F G the second ἐν, before τῇ ἀπολογίᾳ, is omitted. Now intrinsic probability is in favour of the repetition of the ἐν, because there are two distinct specifications, "in my bonds" and "in the defence and confirmation of the Gospel." But the copyist omitted ἐν before τῇ ἀπολογίᾳ, because he did not find it before βεβαιώσει, not observing that it was not needed before that word because βεβαιώσει was included with τῇ ἀπολογίᾳ under one article. Thus transcriptional probability and intrinsic probability concur in favour of the repetition of ἐν.

Again, take the manifest solecism in Phil. 2 : 2, τις σπλάγχνα, which is overwhelmingly supported by all the principal uncials and by nearly all the versions, while the proper, grammatical reading, τινα, appears in only a few minuscules and Fathers. Intrinsic probability is entirely against the attested reading, and transcriptional probability clearly points to a copyist's hasty and careless repetition of τις from the preceding

Causes of unintentional errors.

Concurrence of intrinsic and transcriptional probability.

G

clause. Another instance may be found in Phil. 2 : 15, where the correct reading is ἄμωμα, according to ℵ A B C. But D F G K L P read ἀμώμητά. Paul is citing Deut. 32 : 5. Ἀμώμητος does not occur in the LXX, but μωμητά "blameworthy" appears in that passage. Hence, while it is intrinsically probable that Paul wrote ἄμωμα, it is transcriptionally probable that the scribe, finding μωμητά in the LXX, changed ἄμωμα into ἀμώμητά to correspond.

Scrutiny of separate readings must be supplemented by study of documents as wholes.

But, valuable as this internal evidence for separate readings is, it cannot be trusted by itself. Scrutiny of separate readings must be supplemented by the study of the several documents as wholes. It is fair to assume that the credibility of a reading, however plausible on grounds of intrinsic and transcriptional evidence, may be affected by the general credibility of the document or class of documents in which it appears. It is quite possible that a reading approved by internal evidence should be found in a document or a class of documents which show signs of corruption. That fact would not conclusively discredit the reading, but it would lay it open to suspicion. Let it be constantly borne in mind that we have nothing to do with the doctrinal or other qualities and bearings of the text. The sole object is to reach the text itself in its primitive form. It is a very simple and generally accepted principle that our estimate of the particular details of a book is to be affected and modified by the general character of the book. Any biography of Luther, for instance, may contain truthful details; yet if a question should arise as to the correctness of any detail, our judgment would be inevitably and justly modified by the characteristics of the biography at large. We could not help noting that D'Aubigné deals in wordy panegyric; that Audin betrays strong partisan tendencies; that a distinct theological bias pervades the treatment of Luther by Newman, Bossuet, and Mozley, and that all these are in strong contrast with the sober, dispassionate accuracy of Köstlin. Thus we reach the accepted principle of textual criticism, that knowledge of documents must precede formal judgment on readings.

Knowledge of documents must precede judgment on readings.

This principle requires the student to consider the age of documents and the age of the texts which they contain — two quite distinct questions, since a late document may have been copied from an early text. It is unsafe to estimate the weight of a document by its age alone. Its real weight depends upon the age of its text. This must first be settled by the careful and minute collation of versions and citations, noting all readings which prove themselves to be ancient. Then each manuscript is to be compared with this list of readings, and any manuscript found to contain a considerable proportion of these or of older readings may be noted as containing an ancient text. If we find a number of manuscripts exhibiting a text similar to this, the collected readings of all these will represent, generally, the character of the earlier text.

Weight of documents depends on age of text.

This is a great point gained, yet it still remains to show that this early text is a pure text. The purity of a text does not follow from its early date. We know, for example, that extensive corruptions had found their way into the text of the second century. Accordingly, since our earliest witnesses differ at certain points, we are compelled to push our examination farther, and to test the purity of the text. Here we are thrown back again upon internal evidence, and the only kinds of evidence we have are those already applied to separate readings, namely, intrinsic and transcriptional evidence; only we now apply these two kinds of evidence to whole documents, instead of to individual readings merely. By comparing the readings of two documents in all their variations, we obtain the materials for

An early text not necessarily a pure text.

Intrinsic
and tran-
scriptional
evidence ap-
plied to
documents.
ascertaining the leading merits and defects of each.
There are usually enough readings which strong intrinsic and strong transcriptional probability combine in
attesting, to enable us to reach a sound judgment.
Suppose that we are required to pronounce upon the
comparative textual purity of two documents, represented by T and X. We shall first note all their points
of difference. Next, we shall proceed to discover
which reading, in each case, approves itself as original according to the tests of transcriptional and intrinsic evidence. We thus obtain two lists of readings,
and can easily determine what proportion of original
readings is contained in each. If T shall be found to
contain the larger proportion of preferred readings, and
X to contain habitually the rejected rival readings, we
are entitled to conclude that the text of T has been
transmitted in comparative purity, and that the text
of X has suffered comparatively large corruption. Not
only so, but the purer character of T thus shown may
affect our decision in the case of certain readings preferred in X, and lead us to revise and possibly to
change it. The same process would be pursued if we
had a dozen or fifty or two hundred documents instead of two.

Not reason-
ing in a
circle.
It might be objected, indeed, that we employ the
evidence of separate readings in order to reach our
estimate of the value of the text of a document as a
whole, and that therefore, when it is said that the
relative textual value of each document must be fixed
before we are in a position to decide upon separate
readings, we are reasoning in a circle. But the process by which we determined the value of the document as a whole is tentative. Our general estimate
may be sound, although we may not be able to trust
absolutely all our impressions as to the probabilities
of reading. The general conclusion as to the docu-

ment as a whole does not imply that our estimate of
every separate reading has been correct. In studying
the intrinsic and transcriptional evidence of readings
" we endeavour to deal with each variation separately,
and to decide between its variants immediately, on
the evidence presented by the variation itself in its
context, aided only by general considerations. In the
other case (estimating the comparative textual value
of entire documents) we begin with virtually perform-
ing the same operation, but only tentatively, with a
view to collect materials, not final results; on some
variations we can without rashness predict at this
stage our ultimate conclusions; on many more we can
estimate various degrees of probability; on many
more again, if we are prudent, we shall be content to
remain for the present in entire suspense. Next, we
pass from investigating the readings to investigating
the documents by means of what we have learned
respecting the readings. Thirdly, we return to the
readings, and go once more over the same ground
as at first, but this time making a tentative choice
of readings simply in accordance with documentary
authority." [1]

The results of this comparative criticism applied
to New Testament documents may be illustrated by
Tregelles's classification. (1) Uncials of the most
ancient class, those earlier than the seventh century,
ℵ B D Z. (2) Good later uncials which frequently
accord with these, L X Δ. (3) Important cursives,
generally supporting the most ancient documents, 1,
22, 33, 39, 209. (4) Later uncials.[2]   *(margin: Tregelles's classification of documents.)*

Yet the estimate of the character of documents by
this process is not exhaustive. The problem would
be simpler if each document were homogeneous; but   *(margin: Individual documents not homogeneous.)*

[1] Hort, Introduction, § 40.
[2] *Account of the Printed Text of the New Testament*, 132.

such is not the case. A document may be sound in one part and unsound in another. A manuscript containing several books may have been transcribed from different copies not equally good; or the text of a document may have been compounded of two or more texts of different descent, so that the document has a divided individuality. In such cases a body of readings common to a group of manuscripts represents parts of a manuscript which, for these parts, lay at the root of all the manuscripts in the group. This process of grouping does not account for the combination of the manuscripts. It simply evolves the fact of combination. Criticism, then, goes one step farther, and inquires into the rationale of the combination. It proceeds upon the principle that all trustworthy restoration of corrupted texts is founded on the study of their history; that is, of the relations of descent or affinity which connect the several documents. It classifies documents according to their origin, and arranges the several groups in a genealogical tree, which exhibits their common or proximate origin. "The practice of internal evidence of groups is independent of any genealogical considerations. It proceeds, and must proceed, in utter ignorance of all genealogies. . . . All it knows is, Here are documents united. All it asks is, Do they form a good or a bad combination? Yet, behind internal evidence of groups, the student will see genealogies clamouring for recognition. He notes the peculiarities of the groupings, — some groups frequently occurring, others, apparently equally possible, never occurring at all. He notes the verdicts of internal evidence of groups, — some groups uniformly condemned, others, apparently just like them, almost as uniformly commended. . . . The student would be something other than human if he did not wish to know the cause of all this. And

Criticism investigates the rationale of the combination of documents.

Genealogy of documents.

the hope lies close that all may be explained, and a new and powerful engine of criticism be put into our hands by the investigation of the genealogical affiliations of the manuscripts, which are suggested by these facts. The results of internal evidence of groups suggest not only the study of genealogies, but also certain genealogical facts on which that study may be begun. Every one must suspect that manuscripts that are frequently in company are close of kin. Every one must suspect that the groups which support little else but corruptions are composed of the remaining representatives of a corrupt stock. Everybody must perceive that if such hints are capable of being followed out, and the New Testament documents arranged in accordance with their affiliations, we shall have a means of reaching the true text which will promise more than all other methods combined." [1]

Bengel. — The principle of classifying manuscripts by families was first definitely propounded by John Albrecht Bengel, Superintendent of the Evangelical Lutheran Church of Würtemburg, and widely known to New Testament students by his *Gnomon Novi Testamenti.*

In 1725 Bengel attached to an edition of Chrysostom's *De Sacerdotio* his *Prodromus Novi Testamenti Græci recte cauteque adornandi,* in which he foreshadowed the characteristics of his edition of the New Testament, which appeared in 1734. The title of his New Testament set forth that the text was to exhibit the "marrow" of approved editions, the margin a selection of parallel passages and various readings, distributed into their classes, and the critical apparatus the compendium, supplement, and fruit of sacred criticism, especially Mill's. The text was in

Bengel's Testament.

[1] Professor B. B. Warfield, *Textual Criticism of the New Testament.*

two columns, and the lower margin exhibited various readings in five classes: "genuine, better than the readings in the text, equal to the readings in the text, inferior, not to be approved." The Apparatus Criticus, forming the second part of the work, contained an elaborate dissertation on the Criticism of the New Testament Text. A small edition appeared the same year at Stuttgart, without the critical apparatus. He collated sixteen manuscripts, but not thoroughly. He did not propose to give all the readings of these manuscripts, but only the more important. He stated the evidence for and against each reading.

Bengel clearly perceived that no reliance was to be placed on evidence drawn from the mere numerical majority of readings apart from their origin and character; and that, therefore, witnesses were to be weighed and not counted. He was the first to recognise clearly the importance of the principle of transcriptional probability, viz. that it was more probable that a copyist would try to explain an obscure passage, or to make a hard construction easier, than that he would make difficult what was already easy. Hence his familiar canon, "The difficult is to be preferred to the easy reading" ("Proclivi scriptioni præstat ardua"). The text, arranged in paragraphs, exhibits an intentional departure from the Receptus, marked nevertheless by extreme caution, since he refused to admit, except in the Apocalypse, any reading which had not appeared in one or more preceding editions.

The difficult reading to be preferred to the easy one.

Bengel's chief title to notice as a textualist lies, as already intimated, in his fuller recognition and application of the principle of families of texts; all extant witnesses being thrown into companies, families, tribes, and nations.[1]

---

[1] His own statement of his principle may be seen at length in Scrivener's *Introduction*, II, 212, note.

He divided all extant documents, broadly, into an- Bengel's
cient and modern, under the names African and Asi- families of manu-
atic. The Asiatic proceeded mostly from Constantinople scripts.
and its neighbourhood, and were inferior to the African,
which were fewer, more ancient, and more valuable.
The African he subdivided into two tribes, represented
respectively by A, the only great uncial much known
in his day, and the Old Latin Version. He held that
no Asiatic reading was likely to be genuine unless
supported by some African document. He did not
thoroughly carry out his theory, partly through fear
of exposing the truth to ridicule (" ne risuum periculo
exponatur veritas ").[1]

But one edition of Bengel's New Testament was
issued. His text, however, was frequently reprinted,
and was the standard of the revision of the Authorised
Danish Version, made in 1745 by the authority of the
King of Denmark. Up to the time of his death, in
1752, he continued to enlarge and correct his critical
apparatus, the enlarged edition of which was published, in 1763, under the care of Philip David
Burk. He was particular as to punctuation, and his

---

[1] The list of his codices is as follows : —

Aug. 1 : Evv 83	Dionysianus (ex Johanne Ga-
Aug. 2 : Evv 84	gneio) Act 40 ?
Aug. 3 : Evv 85	Gehl : Evv 89
Aug. 4 : Evrm 24	Hirs : Evv 97
Aug. 5 : Paul 54	Mosc : VEvv
Aug. 6 : Act 46 Paul 55	Par. 10 : (ex Simonio)
Aug. 7 : Apoc. 80	Uff. 1 : Mpaul
Bas. α : EEvv	Uff. vel Uff. 2 : Act 45 Paul 52
Bas. β : Evv 2	Apoc. 16
Bas. γ : Evv 1	Uff. 3 : Evv 101
Byz : Evv 86	Wo. 1 : } ex Wolfio
Cam : Evv (a Joachimo Came-	Wo. 2 : }
rario conlati)	

division into paragraphs was frequently adopted in England.[1]

Wetstein and Semler.—In 1713 John James Wetstein, or Wettstein, Deacon of Basle, prepared a dissertation on Various Readings in the New Testament. In 1716 he met Bentley in England, and at his instance went to Paris in order to collate Codex Ephraemi (C), which he did with great labour and patience. In 1718 he published a specimen of various readings, which brought upon him a charge of Arian and Socinian heresy, and resulted in his deposition and in his expulsion from Basle in 1730.

In the same year his Prolegomena were published anonymously at Amsterdam, giving an outline of his proposed edition of the New Testament and an account of his critical authorities. The edition was described as "acuratissima," derived from the oldest New Testament manuscripts, and treating of the manuscripts of the New Testament, the Greek writers who have made use of it, the ancient versions, the former editors, and the distinguished interpreters; besides "animadversiones et cautiones" for the examination of the various readings of the New Testament.

In 1735 he wrote the preface to a new edition of Gerhard von Maestricht's Greek Testament, in which he referred to the labours of Bengel, for whom he had a

great contempt. He severely reviewed Bengel's Testament immediately upon its appearance, and endeavoured to disparage the critical principles on which

---

[1] See Tischendorf, Prolegomena, 186, 241 f. Scrivener, *Introduction*, II, 210 ff. Hort, Westcott and Hort's *Greek Testament*, Introduction, 180. Tregelles, *Printed Text*, 68–73. Life of Bengel, in the translation of the *Gnomon* by C. T. Lewis and M. R. Vincent, Philadelphia, 1860. J. Chr. Fr. Burk (Bengel's great-grandson), *Johann Albrecht Bengel's Leben und Wirken*, Stuttgart, 1831. Article "Bengel," in Herzog's *Real-Encyklopädie*. E. Nestle, *Bengel als Gelehrter*, Tübingen, 1893.

Bengel had selected his readings, asserting that readings should be adopted which are supported by the greatest number of manuscripts, and entirely ignoring the theory of families.

In 1751–52 appeared his edition of the New Testament, in two volumes folio, with various readings of manuscripts, other editions, Versions, and Fathers; also with a commentary illustrating the history and force of words from ancient writers, — Hebrew, Greek, and Latin. The influence of the Textus Receptus was still apparent, although, in his critical remarks, he laid down the principle that the prescription of the common text should have no authority whatever. His text was the Elzevirian with a few changes. The readings which he preferred, and which amounted to less than five hundred, mostly in the Apocalypse, were placed below the text. It is said that he adopted the Received Text at the request of the Remonstrants or Arminians, whom he had joined on leaving Basle. The various readings were afterward inserted in the text of a Greek Testament published in London, in 1763, by W. Bowyer. Although his Prolegomena of 1730 had announced that his edition was to be derived from the oldest manuscripts, and although he had originally shown a disposition to take Codex A as the basis of his text, his views as to the oldest Greek uncials had evidently undergone a change before the publication of his Testament, in which he attacked the whole body of the older codices under the name of "codices Latinizantes," as being conformed to the Latin Version. Everything in them which agreed with the Latin was denounced as an interpolation from that version.

(margin: Wetstein's Testament.)

But notwithstanding Wetstein's defects, his services to the cause of textual criticism were of great value. The number of manuscripts collated by him was a little over a hundred, and about eleven were examined

(margin: Services to textual criticism.)

for him by others. Besides his own collations, he collected the collations of Mill and others, and reëxamined many of the Versions and Fathers. His collations, though not up to the modern standard of accuracy, were more careful than had been usual. He was the first to investigate the Philoxenian Version. He was superior to Bengel as a collator, and his knowledge of authorities was more extensive; but he was not Bengel's equal in judgment. He was more acute in observing phenomena than accurate in accounting for them. His critical disquisitions were disfigured by the introduction of his personal controversies; but his account of the Versions, Fathers, and early editions was the most extensive and methodical that had ever been published; and his "animadversiones et cautiones" in his second volume were discriminating and valuable.[1]

Semler edits Wetstein's Prolegomena. Wetstein's Prolegomena were reprinted at Halle, in 1765, by Johann Salomo Semler, Professor of Theology at Halle. Semler was the leader of the reaction in Germany against the traditional views of the canon of Scripture. His edition of Wetstein bore the title, *Wetstenii Libelli ad Crisin et Interpretationem Novi Testamenti.* It contained notes and remarks of his own, with facsimiles of manuscripts. He defended the Græco-Latin codices against Wetstein's charges. Still later, in 1831, the Prolegomena were issued in a condensed form by J. A. Lotze, Rotterdam.

Expands Bengel's theory of families. Semler took up Bengel's theory of families and expanded it. He was the first to apply the term "Recension" to the ancient texts, an error which has caused some confusion. A Recension is properly a work of criticism by editors; but it is used, even by some modern critics, as synonymous with "family."[2]

---

[1] A summary of the principal points is given by Tregelles, *Printed Text,* 79 f.

[2] See Tregelles, *Printed Text,* 84.

Semler classified manuscripts, at first, under two "Recensions": (1) Oriental, or that of Lucian; (2) Western or Egypto-Palestinian, and that of Origen, agreeing with the Itala, the Memphitic, and the Armenian. The Vulgate, he thought, proceeded from a less ancient text. In 1767 he made three recensions : (1) Alexandrian, used by the Egyptian writers, the pupils of Origen, and the Syriac, Memphitic, and Ethiopic Versions; (2) Oriental, used at Antioch and Constantinople; (3) Western. In the later codices he thought that all the recensions were mixed. Like Bengel, he insisted that codices were to be weighed and not numbered.[1]

A review of the first period exhibits, in the beginning, a scarcity of documentary sources, an arbitrary determination of the text on a false and narrow basis, and a general ignorance of the comparative value of documents. The small number of manuscripts accessible or used was only one of the obstacles which opposed the purification of the text. Scholars were unable to make the best choice from among those actually at hand, or were not accurate in comparing them, or estimated the value of readings according to their number. "In consequence of the astonishing number of copies which appeared at the very begin-

Review of the first period.

Obstacles.

---

[1] Semler's editorial work on Wetstein is sharply criticised by Tregelles, *Printed Text*, 82.

On Wetstein : Tischendorf, Prolegomena, 243 ff. C. R. Hagenbach, J. J. Wetstein der Kritiker und seine Gegner, *Zeitschr. für d. histor. Theologie*, Leipzig, 1839, Bd. IX, fasc. 1. Tregelles, *Printed Text*, 73–82. Carl Bertheau, article "Wettstein," Herzog's *Real-Encyklopädie*.

On Semler : Tischendorf, Prolegomena, 187. A. Tholuck's article "Semler," in Herzog's *Real-Encyklopädie*, rev. by Tzschirner. J. S. Semler, *Hermeneutische Vorbereitung*, Halle, 1765. Id., *Apparatus ad Liberalem N. T. Interpretationem*, Halle, 1767.

ning, in a long series of manual editions, mostly from one and the same recension, the idea grew up spontaneously very early that in the manuscripts also the text was tolerably uniform, and that any thorough revision of it was unnecessary and impertinent. The Oriental Versions were closed to most; the importance of the Church Fathers was scarcely suspected; but the greatest lack of all for the purification of the text was the indispensable knowledge of the process of its corruption " (Reuss). Moreover, the beginning of the seventeenth century was marked by the rise of the Purist controversy. The Purists maintained that to deny that God gave the New Testament in anything but pure classical Greek was to imperil the doctrine of inspiration. The Wittemberg Faculty, in 1638, decreed that to speak of barbarisms or solecisms in the New Testament was blasphemy against the Holy Ghost. Hence, a correct conception of the peculiar idiom of the Apostles was impossible, and the estimate of different readings was seriously affected by this cause. Readings of existing editions were arbitrarily mingled, the manuscripts employed and the sources of variants adopted were not properly specified, and a full survey of the apparatus was impossible.[1]

The number of uncial sources, however, gradually increased; the existence of various readings was recognised, but they were merely registered, and not applied to the construction of a purer text. There

Purist controversy.

[1] A useful table, showing the dates at which the extant Greek uncials of the sixth and earlier centuries, with five others of later date but comparatively ancient text, have become available as evidence from 1550 down to 1880, may be found in Dr. Hort's Introduction to Westcott and Hort's Greek Testament, 14, 15. The table exhibits the dates of imperfect publication by selection of readings, of tolerably full collations, and of continuous texts.

began to be signs of revolt against the authority of the Textus Receptus and attempts to restore the text on the evidence of manuscript readings. There arose a growing distrust of the numerical basis of evidence. Manuscripts began to be weighed instead of counted. There was a dawning recognition of the value of ancient documents and a corresponding effort to formulate principles of classification. A large mass of material, relating to manuscripts, Fathers, and Versions, was collected, which awaited thorough sifting and arrangement, and the doctrine of families of texts was broached. Through all the Received Text substantially maintained its supremacy, though its pretensions were boldly challenged by individual critics; its chain was rudely shaken and more than once broken, and its authority began to be visibly weakened.

For twenty years after the appearance of Wetstein's edition little progress was made in the arrangement and application of the large accumulations, and no attempt to carry out the suggestions of Bentley, Bengel, and Semler respecting the classification of documents. In England, the attention of students was directed to the study of the Hebrew Scriptures. The superstitious hesitancy about departing from the Received Text still prevailed, and the critical valuation of the older uncials was suffering seriously from Wetstein's sweeping charge of latinisation.

CHAPTER X

THE SECOND PERIOD: TRANSITION FROM THE
TEXTUS RECEPTUS TO THE OLDER UNCIAL
TEXT (1770–1830). GRIESBACH

Points of advance in the second period inaugurated by Griesbach.

In studying this period we shall observe an enlarged comparison of the three sources of the text and an issue of critical canons. We shall see that the dominion of the Textus Receptus is not overthrown, but that that text is gradually improved, and that there is a growing departure from it in the direction of an older and better text.

The great name which marks the real inauguration of this period is that of John Jacob Griesbach, 1745–1812; but before considering his work, something should be said of several others from whose labours he derived valuable aid.

Harwood.

In 1776 Edward Harwood, of London, issued an edition, applying the Codex Cantabrigiensis (D) in the Gospels and Acts, the Codex Claromontanus (D₂) in the Pauline Epistles, and the Codex Alexandrinus (A) where these were wanting. He departed considerably from the Elzevir text, and presented a number of new readings, many of which are approved by modern critics.

Matthæi.

Christian Frederic Matthæi, a Thuringian, was Professor at Wittemberg and afterward at Moscow, where he found a quantity of Greek manuscripts, both biblical and patristic, originally brought from Mt.

Athos, uncollated, and almost entirely unknown in Western Europe.[1]

From these materials he prepared an edition of the New Testament, the first volume of which was published at Riga in 1782, and the remainder at intervals during the next six years. The whole formed twelve thin volumes, each containing a preface, with facsimiles of manuscripts. The Greek text was accompanied with a Latin Version. His second edition, in three volumes, 1803–1807, omitted the Latin Version and most of the critical notes. In this edition he speaks of having made collations of fresh manuscripts, but these have disappeared. With good scholarship, he was ignorant of critical principles and of what had been accomplished by former editors, not having seen, when he began, the editions of either Mill or Wetstein. He was unable to estimate the comparative value of codices. He was a laborious and thorough collator, but a poor critic. His prefaces were devoid of arrangement, and his judgments were warped by a hasty temper, which vented itself especially upon Griesbach. He utterly repudiated the theory of families of texts, decried the evidence of patristic citations, and seconded Wetstein in his depreciation of the earliest manuscripts. His test of the value of manuscripts was their agreement with those current in later times. The manuscripts on which his text was based were of inferior value, belonging to the family which Bengel had styled "Asiatic," and which Griesbach called "Constantinopolitan." His only claim to notice lies in his excellence as a collator.[2]

Character as a critic.

---

[1] To him solely we are indebted for Evan. V, 237–259 ; Acts 98–107 ; P. 113–124 ; Ap. 47–50 ; nearly all at Moscow. Full list in Tischendorf, Prolegomena, 249 f.

[2] See Tischendorf, Prolegomena, 249 f. Scrivener, *Introduction*, II, 216–219. Tregelles, *Printed Text*, 85.

H

Francis Karl Alter, a Jesuit of Silesia, was Professor of Greek at Vienna. His edition of the New Testament in two volumes, 8vo, Vienna, 1786–87, was founded on a manuscript in the Imperial Library at Vienna (Evan. 218, Acts 65, P. 57, Ap. 83), which had some value, but was not remarkable nor ancient. This he printed at full length, correcting scribal errors by Stephen's edition of 1546, and collating with his text twenty-one other manuscripts from the Vienna Library. He added readings from the Coptic Version, from four Slavonic Codices, and from one Latin Codex.[1]

Christian VII, King of Denmark, employed to examine manuscripts in different countries a company consisting of Andrew Birch, a Lutheran bishop in Denmark, Jacob G. C. Adler, D. G. Moldenhauer, and O. G. Tychsen, a distinguished Orientalist. Their labours were confined principally to Spain and Italy, and occupied several years. The results were edited

by Birch in his folio edition of the Four Gospels, Copenhagen, 1788. The text was Stephen's, 1550, to which were added the various readings collected by the company, descriptive prolegomena, and facsimiles. The readings of B were now published for the first time, partly from Birch's own collation, and partly from that made for Bentley. The completion of the edition was prevented by a fire in the printing-house in 1795. The various readings collected for the Acts and Epistles were issued in 1798, and those for the Apocalypse in 1800. In 1801 the readings accompanying the text of the Gospels were revised, reëdited, and printed in a form to correspond with the portions already issued. Tregelles says that Birch probably did more than any other scholar in the collation of

---

[1] See Tischendorf, Prolegomena, 254. Scrivener, *Introduction*, II, 220.

manuscripts of the New Testament; and Scrivener speaks in high terms of his conscientiousness and appreciation of the difficulties of his task, and remarks that he was almost the first to open to us the literary treasures of the Vatican, of Florence, and of Venice. Quite different was the work of Moldenhauer and Tychsen in Spain, which was performed in a slovenly and superficial manner, principally because of their dislike for Spain and its religion. *Work of Moldenhauer and Tychsen.*

While, as already remarked, little if anything was done for twenty years after Wetstein by way of applying the accumulations of himself and of his predecessors, the work of accumulation was not arrested. Besides the collections of Matthæi and Birch, the texts of several important documents were printed, among them the New Testament portion of A, edited by Woide in 1786. Kipling published Codex D in 1793, and Matthæi edited the Greek and Latin Codex G of Paul's Epistles (Bœrnerianus, ninth century). Griesbach, therefore, had the advantage of larger collections than those left by Wetstein. In the twenty years between the first edition of Griesbach and the first volume of his second edition, the materials had increased to double the quantity previously known. *Important texts printed and edited.*

Griesbach was a native of Hesse Darmstadt and a pupil of Semler. He was, for a short time, Professor of Divinity at Halle, and afterward at Jena. In 1774 he issued the first part of a Greek New Testament in which the first Three Gospels were arranged synoptically. The Fourth Gospel and Acts appeared in 1775, and also the volume containing the Epistles and the Apocalypse. In 1777 the first part of the work was reprinted with the Gospels in the usual order. This portion, with the issues of 1775, form Griesbach's first edition. The critical materials were drawn largely from Wetstein, but he made independent additions. *J. J. Griesbach. His first edition.*

He did not adopt many new readings, and the Received Text, while not wholly followed, was taken as a basis.[1] He gave a number of readings in the margin, classified according to families.

Symbolæ Criticæ and the second edition of the New Testament.

His *Symbolæ Criticæ*, two volumes, 1785, 1793, further prepared the way for his second edition. This had behind it twenty years of wider study, besides the work of Harwood, Matthæi, Birch, Alter, and others. The first volume appeared in 1796, the second in 1806. His critical apparatus was larger than in the first edition. In his preface he laid down his principles of criticism and dealt with the history of the text. He had studied the readings in Origen, had inspected Codices A and D of the Gospels, and had carefully examined C. Besides these he had consulted twenty-six manuscripts of the Gospels, ten of the Acts, fifteen of Paul, and one of the Apocalypse, with twelve Lectionaries of the Gospels, and two of the Apostles. He did not exhibit all the results of his own collations nor of those of his predecessors, his purpose being to use their material for the illustration of his own principles, and thus to help students to independent conclusions concerning readings. In 1805, the year before the issue of his second volume, he published a manual edition containing the text and the more important various readings, but without giving the authorities for the readings. This edition, differing in some places from the larger work, represents his matured and final conclusions on the New Testament text.

Manual edition.

Critical conditions confronting Griesbach.

With Griesbach, really critical texts may be said to have begun. The critical conditions which confronted him were these: A vast mass of material had been accumulated; many manuscripts and versions had been examined, but the examination had been partial; the

---

[1] For details, see Tischendorf, Prolegomena, 246.

suggestions of Bengel and Bentley concerning the classification of manuscripts had been disregarded; there was
still much hesitancy about departing from the Received
Text; Wetstein's depreciation of the character of the
most ancient codices had taken effect, and had greatly
impaired the sense of their value. The task which
lay before Griesbach was to vindicate the authority of
the older codices, to classify authorities, and to use
them critically and consistently for the restoration of
the text.

He took issue with Wetstein on the value of the His views of
ancient manuscripts, and followed in the track of ancient
Bentley, Bengel, and Semler. He adopted the family- and fami-
theory, holding, with Bengel, a twofold division, — lies.
Asiatic or Byzantine and African, but, like Semler,
dividing the African into two parts, thus making three
classes, two ancient, and one later. These he denom-
inated Western, Alexandrian, and Constantinopolitan.
The Western, with its numerous glosses, represented
the text which had been in circulation in the earlier
times, but which, owing to the errors of copyists, required much correction. The Alexandrian was an
attempt to revise this text, and was marked by corrections of grammar and style. The Constantinopolitan,
Bengel's Asiatic, flowed from the other two. The
Western and Alexandrian existed as distinct in the
latter part of the second century. The standard of
the Alexandrian text was Origen. To that family
would belong A, B, C, L (Gospels), and the Egyptian
and some minor Versions. To the Western family
would belong D (Gospels and Acts) and other ancient
copies containing a Latin translation, the Old Latin
and Vulgate, and the Latin Fathers. The Constantinopolitan embraced the great majority of manuscripts,
with the larger proportion of Versions and patristic
writings. In deciding on a reading he relied chiefly

on the evidence furnished by union of families. The agreement of the Western and Alexandrian he regarded as particularly important, often decisive. Thus, in Matt. 19:17, he read τί με ἐρωτᾷς περὶ τοῦ ἀγαθοῦ; " Why askest thou me concerning the good ? " instead of τί με λέγεις ἀγαθόν; "Why callest thou me good ? " on the joint evidence of B D L, the Old Latin and the Vulgate. In this reading he is followed by Westcott and Hort and Tischendorf, and the testimony of אַ, which, of course, he did not know, has been added to that of his other manuscripts.

Griesbach's critical canons.   Among the critical canons laid down by Griesbach are the following: (1) No reading must be considered preferable, unless it has the support of at least some ancient testimonies. (2) All criticism of the text turns on the study of recensions or classes of documents. Not single documents but recensions are to be counted in determining readings. (3) The shorter reading is to be preferred to the longer. This canon rests on the well-known tendency of scribes to amplify the text, and to include in it all marginal notes, glosses, etc. It was probably in this way that the episode of John 8 : 1–11, and the legend of the angel troubling the waters of the pool of Bethzatha, John 5 : 4, slipped into the text. If a shorter reading is elliptical, obscure, or harsh, it is not unlikely that the copyist may have felt it to be his duty to fill out the ellipsis, or to add some words in order to render it less obscure or smoother. (4) The more difficult reading is to be preferred to the easier. This canon was first laid down by Bengel. It grows out of the tendency of copyists to alter what they did not understand into something which they did understand. A scribe might be puzzled by a solecism, or by the irregular use of a word, or by a Hebraism, or by a want of connexion, and, in entire good faith, change the reading so as to make it, as he thought, more intelligible. Thus may probably be explained, in Matt. 6 : 1, the change of δικαιοσύνην, "righteousness," into ἐλεημοσύνην, "alms"; and of ἁμαρτήματος, "sin," in Mark 3 : 29, into κρίσεως, "judgment." (5) Along with this canon and included in it goes the canon that the reading which, at first sight, appears to convey a false sense, is to be preferred to other readings. Thus, in 1 Cor. 11 : 29, ἀναξίως, "unworthily," is omitted by the best texts. Reading the text with this omission, the first impression would be that the verse absolutely affirms that he that eats and drinks does not discern the Lord's body, and therefore incurs judgment. The difficulty vanishes when the proper conditional force is given to μὴ, and we read, "He that eateth and drinketh, eateth and drinketh judgment to himself *if he do not* discern (or distinguish) the body." Probably the scribe, not appreciating the conditional force of μὴ, and being staggered by his false impression of the statement, imported ἀναξίως into the passage from ver. 27.

The line of distinction which Griesbach drew between Alexandrian and Western it was impossible to maintain. On this point he virtually abandoned his former conclusion. In his "Commentarius Criticus," 1811, he showed that the readings of Origen do not accord precisely with the Alexandrian Recension to which he had assigned them. Indeed, the practical weight of his whole system of recensions was impaired by his own declaration that in none of the existing codices is a recension contained in its purity. In several, and those our oldest manuscripts, a difference of recension is apparent in the individual parts. A, for example, follows one recension in the Gospels, another in the Pauline Epistles, and still another in the Acts and Catholic Epistles. The term "Western" was misapplied, since this type of text is not confined

[margin:] Abandoned the distinction between Alexandrian and Western.

to the West.[1] Moreover, the manuscripts on which the Textus Receptus is based belong to the Byzantine family, so that Griesbach's scanty respect for that family was not consistent with the deference paid in his edition to the Textus Receptus. He did not really take as his textual basis the ancient texts in which he professed the most confidence. He did not take the decisive step of entirely disregarding the Textus Receptus, and forming a text resting on the best authorities throughout.[2]

Griesbach's text is the basis of many manual editions, as those of Schott, Märker, Knapp, Tittmann, Hahn, and Theile. Hahn's was republished at New York, in 1842, by Dr. Edward Robinson.[3]

[1] See G. Salmon, *Some Criticism of the Text of the New Testament*, 46 ff.

[2] The critical discussion of Griesbach's classification may be studied in Hort's Introduction to Westcott and Hort's *Greek Testament*, 183, and in Scrivener's *Introduction*, II, 224 ff. Dr. Hort, while criticising Griesbach's conclusions, expresses himself as venerating the name of Griesbach above that of every other textual critic of the New Testament. He says, "What Bengel had sketched tentatively, was verified and worked out with admirable patience, sagacity, and candor by Griesbach, who was equally great in independent investigation and in his power of estimating the results arrived at by others." Tregelles says that though his later critical edition is more complete, and in all respects more valuable, yet, if his system of recensions in its application is the subject of examination, the first edition is necessary (*Printed Text*, 84).

[3] See Tischendorf, Prolegomena, 188 ff., 246 ff. Scrivener, *Introduction*, II, 216, 222-226. Tregelles, *Printed Text*, 83-85, 88-92. Hort, Introduction to Westcott and Hort's *Greek Testament*, 181-186. Reuss, *Bibliotheca Novi Testamenti*, 193-204, and article "Griesbach," in Herzog's *Real-Encyklopädie*. Augusti, *Über Griesbach's Verdienste*, Breslau, 1812. R. Laurence, *Remarks on the Systematical Classification of Manuscripts adopted by Griesbach in his Edition of the Greek Testament*, Oxford, 1814. O. von Gebhardt, article "Bibeltext," in Herzog's *Real-Encyklopädie*.

CHAPTER XI

THE SECOND PERIOD (1770-1830). THE SUCCESSORS OF GRIESBACH

J. L. Hug (1765-1846), a Roman Catholic Professor at Freiburg, in his *Einleitung in die Schriften des Neuen Testament*, 1808, proposed, as a corrective of the views of Bengel and Griesbach, a new system of recensions. According to him, the text, in the general mass of codices, had degenerated, by the middle of the third century, into the form exhibited in Codex Bezæ (D) of the Gospels, the Old Latin, Sahidic, and to some extent the Peshitto Versions, and in the citations of Clement of Alexandria and of Origen in his earlier works. To this text he gave the name κοινὴ ἔκδοσις, "common edition." He supposed that it received three separate revisions in the middle of the third century,—one by Origen, adopted by Jerome, and two others, by Hesychius in Egypt, and Lucian in Antioch, both which Jerome condemned, and Pope Gelasius (492-96) declared to be apocryphal.[1] His views were adopted, with some modifications, notably the rejection of the Origenian Revision, by J. G. Eichhorn, *Einleitung in das Neue Testament*, Leipzig, 1827. The theory has been shown to be baseless, though it "brought out the fact of the early broad currency of the Western Text" (Warfield).[2]

Hug proposes a new system of recensions.

[1] See Tischendorf, Prolegomena, 194.
[2] It found, however, a feeble resurrectionist and defender a few years ago, in Dr. G. W. Samson, *The English Revisers'*

Hug on
Codex B.

It should be added, however, that to Hug's *De Antiquitate Vaticani Codicis Commentatio*, 1810, is due the merit of first placing that document in its true rank. His conclusion as to its date is generally accepted by modern critics.[1]

Scholz. — The backward movement of Matthæi was seconded by John Martin Augustine Scholz, Roman Catholic Dean of Theology in the mixed University of Bonn, and a pupil of Hug. He was an extensive

Scholz, as
collector
and collator.

traveller, and collected in his journeys a vast amount of fresh material which appeared in his *Curæ Criticæ in Historiam Textus Evangeliorum*, Heidelberg, 1820; his *Biblisch-kritische Reise*, Leipzig, 1823; and his *Novum Testamentum Græce*, 4to, Leipzig, 1830, 1836.[2]

The number of codices registered by him for the first time was 616, of which, however, he collated entire only thirteen. Scrivener says, "His inaccuracy in the description of manuscripts which he must have had before him when he was writing is most wearisome to those who have had to trace his steps, and to verify or rather falsify his statements."[3]

Scholz frequently departed from the Textus Recep-

Greek Text shown to be unauthorised except by Egyptian Copies discarded by Greeks, and to be opposed to the Historic Text of All Ages and Churches, Cambridge, Mass. Dr. Schaff characterises the treatise as "a curious anachronism."

[1] See Tischendorf, Prolegomena, 192. Tregelles, *Printed Text*, 90. Scrivener, *Introduction*, II, 270–272. Hort, Introduction to Westcott and Hort's *Greek Testament*, 181–183.

[2] For details of Scholz's collections, see Tischendorf, Prolegomena, 630–638, 659–665, 679–681, 702–714, 943–945.

[3] Dr. C. R. Gregory (Prolegomena to Tischendorf, 192) describes him as "Itineribus præclarior quam doctrina, codicum conlator neglegentissimus." Compare 257. Burgon speaks of him as "an incorrigible blunderer." But Dr. Gregory, in a recent lecture at Union Seminary, spoke in commendatory terms of Scholz, and asserted that he was a more careful collator than Scrivener.

tus, and yet, on the whole, preserved it in preference to that of the Vulgate. In many passages in which Griesbach had varied from the Textus Receptus, on the ground of the antiquity of the authorities, Scholz followed more recent documents on the evidence of number, thus adhering to readings of the Received Text.

He at first divided documents into five families,—two African (Alexandrian and Western), one Asiatic, one Byzantine, and one Cyprian. Later he adopted Bengel's classification, and maintained that the true text was to be sought in the Constantinopolitan family, claiming that this family had always presented one uniform text, which had become traditional throughout the Greek Church. This text had been preserved without serious corruption before Constantinople became the seat of empire, had retained its general purity in the fourth century, and was retained and transmitted in the Patriarchate of Constantinople. He maintained the general unity in text of the Constantinopolitan manuscripts, as against the mutual discrepancies of the Alexandrian manuscripts and Versions. According to his classification, then, the Alexandrian family would embrace the most ancient manuscripts, the Old Latin, Jerome's Vulgate, the two Egyptian and the Ethiopic Versions. The Constantinopolitan would include the later manuscripts generally, a part of the Old Syriac, the later Syriac, Gothic, Georgian, and Slavonic Versions, and certain Fathers from the fourth century onward. His system thus differed from Griesbach's by the inclusion of Griesbach's Western family in the Alexandrian, and by assigning the preference to the Constantinopolitan, which, according to Griesbach, was a resultant of the Western and Alexandrian.[1]

Scholz's system of families.

[1] Tregelles says, *Printed Text*, 152 : "Scholz's first volume was published in 1830. The second did not appear till

Scholz's error in assuming a standard Constantinopolitan text.

Careful examination would have shown Scholz the contrary of what he took for granted, namely, the existence of a standard, public, authorised Constantinopolitan text. Scrivener has shown that the more modern copies do not contain a uniform text, and that, "with certain points of general resemblance, whereby they are distinguished from the older documents of the Alexandrian class, they abound with mutual variations so numerous and perpetual as to vouch for the independent origin of nearly all of them." [1]

Character of Scholz's services.

Scholz's services consisted mainly in pointing out the localities of manuscripts. The greater part of the documents which he was the first to consult were recorded in his list, but their readings did not appear in his collection of variants.

The gravitation of his text toward the Textus Receptus made it popular with conservative critics who

1836. Prior to that year I made a particular examination, in the Gospels, of those readings which he rejects in his inner margin as Alexandrian; in the course of this examination, and with continued reference to the authorities which he cited, I observed what a remarkable body of witnesses stood in opposition to the text which he had adopted as Constantinopolitan. Thus I learned that the most ancient manuscripts were witnesses against his text; and not only so, but when I sought to ascertain the character of these manuscripts themselves, I found that they were continually supported by many of the older versions. While engaged in this examination, I went all through St. Matthew's Gospel, writing in the margin of a Greek Testament those well-supported readings which Scholz rejected. This was, of course, wholly for my own use; but I saw that, as a general principle, the modern manuscripts can have no authority apart from ancient evidence, and that it is the ancient manuscripts alone (although comparatively few in number) which show within what limits we have to look as to the real ancient text."

[1] See also Hort, Introduction to Westcott and Hort's *Greek Testament*, 144.

hesitated at Griesbach's conclusions, and it found many friends in England. Later (1845), Scholz retracted his preference for the Constantinopolitan text, and declared that if a new edition of his Greek Testament should be called for, he would receive into the text most of the Alexandrian readings which he had placed in his margin.[1]

"Through these years (1770–1830)," says Dr. C. R. Gregory, "the controversy was between the adherents of the Received Text and those who preferred to trust the ancient witnesses. Harwood alone rejected the Receptus, and he was rejected by his peers. Others, even Griesbach, showed the futility of holding the Textus Receptus as a foundation for the construction of a text. At this point we bid farewell to the Textus Receptus without regret: a new day is dawning — the day which seeks the ancient text without hindrance from the tradition of later ages."

Farewell to the Textus Receptus.

---

[1] See Tischendorf, Prolegomena, 192, 193, 255–257. Scrivener, *Introduction*, II, 226–230. Tregelles, *Printed Text*, 92–97, 179 ff. J. Scott Porter, *Principles of Textual Criticism*, Belfast, 1848. F. H. A. Scrivener, *A Full and Exact Collation of about Twenty Greek Manuscripts of the Holy Gospels* (hitherto unexamined) *deposited in the British Museum, the Archiepiscopal Library at Lambeth, etc., with a Critical Introduction*, Cambridge, 1853.

CHAPTER XII

THIRD PERIOD (1830–81). EFFORTS FOR THE RES-
TORATION OF THE PRIMITIVE TEXT. LACH-
MANN

A NEW period began in 1831, when, for the first
time, a text was constructed directly from the ancient
documents without the intervention of any printed
edition, and when the first systematic attempt was
made to substitute scientific method for arbitrary
choice in the discrimination of various readings. To

Lachmann casts aside the Textus Receptus. Carl Lachmann belongs the distinction of entirely
casting aside the Textus Receptus, and placing the
New Testament text wholly on the basis of actual
authority. Lachmann boldly adopted Bentley's principle that the entire text is to be formed apart from
the influence of printed editions, on evidence. Dr.
Warfield remarks that if Bentley had completed his
edition, he would have antedated the step of Lachmann by a century.

Carl Lachmann was Professor of Classical Philology
in Berlin. He was not a professional theologian, but
a philologist, who had distinguished himself by critical
editions of Latin and German classics.[1]

Lachmann's first New Testament. In 1831 he published a small edition of the Greek
Testament, with a brief notice of his plan, followed by
a list of the places in which his readings differed from

[1] His edition of Lucretius still ranks among standards. A
fourth edition of the text was issued in 1871, and of the Commentary in 1882.

those of the common text, and referring the reader for further information to his article in the *Studien und Kritiken*, (1830, No. 4, 817–845). He declared that he had followed the usage of the most ancient Oriental churches; that where this was not uniform he had preferred what was supported by the consensus of African and Italian authorities; that where there was great uncertainty it was indicated partly by enclosing words within brackets, and partly by placing a different reading in the margin, the so-called Textus Receptus being allowed no place.

His larger edition, *Novum Testamentum Græce et Latine*, was published in two volumes at Berlin, 1842–50. In this he was aided by the younger Philip Buttmann, who added the critical apparatus of the Greek text, and also published a small edition based on the Codex Vaticanus (1856, 1862, 1865). **Larger edition.**

Lachmann recognised only two types of text: Oriental (A, B, C, Origen) and Occidental (D, E, F, G, oldest Latin Versions, Vulgate, and Western Fathers from Irenæus down to Primasius for the Apocalypse). He entirely disregarded Byzantine authorities and the Syriac and Egyptian Versions. **His types of text.**

The text of the larger edition did not vary greatly from that of the earlier. Only the text of the smaller edition was wholly based on the sources which he styled "Oriental," while in the larger, he used the combined evidence of Eastern and Western authorities.

His object was purely historical, that is, to present the text in the form in which the most ancient documents, so far as these were known, had transmitted it. His text was not put forth as the original or final text, but as the oldest attainable text, namely, that of the fourth century, as an historical basis for further inquiries which might lead nearer to the primitive text. **His aim not the original but the oldest attainable text.**

Rules for estimating comparative weight of readings.

He laid down six rules for estimating the comparative weight of readings: (1) Nothing is better attested than that in which all authorities agree. (2) The agreement has less weight if part of the authorities are silent or in any way defective. (3) The evidence for a reading, when it is that of witnesses of different regions, is greater than that of the witnesses of some particular place, differing either from negligence or from set purpose. (4) The testimonies are to be regarded as doubtfully balanced when witnesses from widely separated regions stand opposed to others equally wide apart. (5) Readings are uncertain which occur habitually in different forms in different regions. (6) Readings are of weak authority which are not uniformly attested in the same region.

Lachmann's use of the terms "Eastern" and "Western."

With Griesbach, Lachmann distinguished between Eastern and Western witnesses; but the peculiar sense in which he used those terms caused his meaning to be misapprehended. Others had used the term "Oriental" or "Asiatic" to denote the mass of the more recent manuscripts gathered from the churches of Syria, Asia Minor, and Constantinople, containing the text which had, perhaps, originally come into use in the regions from Antioch to Constantinople, and classed by Griesbach as "Byzantine." Lachmann meant by "Eastern" the few ancient codices comprised in Griesbach's Alexandrian class. His witnesses were, for the Gospels A, B, C, the fragments P, Q, T, Z, sometimes D. For the Acts, D, E₂. For Paul, D₂, G₂, H₃. With these the citations of Origen, the Greek remains of Irenæus, the Old Latin manuscripts a, b, c, and the citations from Cyprian, Hilary of Poitiers, Lucifer of Cagliari, and Primasius.[1]

---

[1] The following will explain the notations of those of Lachmann's authorities which may be less familiar: —

P, Codex Guelpherbytanus, sixth century, Wolfenbüttel, 518

Through almost a quarter of the New Testament Lachmann had scarcely any means of deciding how far the Eastern witnesses varied in readings. There are passages in which at most two manuscripts, or perhaps only one, contain the text. Thus an error in such a copy or copies is assumed to be a widely spread reading of the fourth century. It is to be remembered, further, that at that time neither B nor C had been thoroughly examined. Where his Eastern witnesses disagreed, he had recourse to Western sources; and, these failing, to sources of inferior age and authority.

It is thus evident that his method was too rigid, and the range of his authorities too limited; and it is not strange that his text was regarded as an innovation, and treated accordingly. If his exposition of his plan and object had been fuller and simpler, his work might have met with a better reception. As it is, " Let any objections be raised to the plan, let inconsistencies be pointed out in the execution, let corrections of varied kinds be suggested, still the fact will remain that the first Greek Testament, since the invention of printing, edited wholly on ancient authority, irrespective of modern traditions, is due to Charles Lachmann " (Tregelles). *His method too rigid.*

He bestowed great pains in editing the Latin Version of Jerome, which was added to his Greek text. His principal authorities were the Codex Fuldensis (sixth century), which he and Buttmann studied *Great pains bestowed on Jerome's Latin Version.*

vv. of the Gospels. Q, Codex Guelpherbytanus II, fifth century, palimpsest, Wolfenbüttel, 247 vv. of Luke and John. T, Codex Borgianus I, fifth century, College of the Propaganda at Rome, fragments of Luke and John, Greek text with Sahidic or Thebaic Version. Z, Codex Dublinensis, sixth century, palimpsest, Matthew. E₂, Codex Laudianus, sixth century, Bodleian Library, Oxford, Acts. G₂, Acts, seventh century, St. Petersburg. H₃, Codex Coislinianus, sixth century, fragments distributed in different libraries, Pauline Epistles.

I

together at Fulda in 1839, and the Codex Amiatinus (sixth century) of the Laurentian Library at Florence, a description of which may be found in Scrivener's *Introduction*, II, 71. Of this codex he had only an imperfect collation. With these and some other aid from manuscripts he revised the whole of Jerome's Version. In his preface he gave some valuable matter on the subject of the Latin texts. He held that the Old Latin proceeded from Northern Africa, and that its text had been modernised into a form resembling the later Greek manuscripts.[1]

[1] The following table exhibits a few of Lachmann's readings, compared with those of the Textus Receptus and Westcott and Hort : —

	REC.	LACH.^N	W. H.
Matt. 21 : 31 :	ὁ πρῶτος	ὁ ὕστερος	ὁ ὕστερος
Luke 2 : 14 :	εὐδοκία	εὐδοκίας	εὐδοκίας
Luke 7 : 31 :	εἶπε δὲ ὁ Κύριος	Omit	Omit
John 3 : 15 :	μὴ ἀπόληται ἀλλ'	[μὴ ἀπόληται ἀλλ']	Omit
John 8 : 84 :	ἐκ μέτρου δίδωσιν ὁ θεὸς	ἐκ μέτρου δίδωσιν [ὁ θεὸς]	ἐκ μέτρου δίδωσιν
John 6 : 22 :	ἐκεῖνο εἰς ὃ ἐνέβησαν οἱ μαθηταὶ αὐτοῦ	Omit	Omit
John 6 : 51 :	ἣν ἐγὼ δώσω	Omit	Omit
Acts 13 : 33 :	τῷ δευτέρῳ	τῷ πρώτῳ	τῷ δευτέρῳ
Rom. 1 : 29 :	πορνείᾳ	Omit	Omit
Rom. 5 : 1 :	ἔχομεν	ἔχωμεν (mg)	ἔχωμεν
Rom. 5 : 2 :	τῇ πίστει	[ ]	[ ]
Rom. 7 : 25 :	εὐχαριστῶ	χάρις	χάρις
1 Cor. 11 : 29 :	ἀναξίως	Omit	Omit
Eph. 1 : 15 :	τὴν ἀγάπην	Omit	Omit
Eph. 2 : 21 :	πᾶσα ἡ οἰκοδομὴ	Omit ἡ	Omit ἡ
Heb. 10 : 84 :	δεσμοῖς	δεσμίοις	δεσμίοις
Apoc. 18 : 3 :	πέπωκε	πέπωκαν	πέπτωκαν

See Hort, Introduction to Westcott and Hort's *Greek Testament*, 13. Lachmann's Life, by Hertz, Berlin, 1851. Tischendorf, Prolegomena, 193, 258–366. Tregelles, *Printed Text*, 97–117. Scrivener, *Introduction*, II, 231–235. O. von Gebhardt, article " Bibeltext," in Herzog's *Real-Encyklopädie*.

The editions of Hahn (1840, 1861) and Theile (1844), based on the Textus Receptus, but giving many readings from Griesbach, and some from Lachmann and Tischendorf, did nothing to promote Textual Criticism beyond giving wider currency to the new readings. The successive editions of Dr. Samuel Thomas Bloomfield, published in England and America (1832–43), merely testify to the lack of the critical art at that time and in those countries.[1] Equally without critical value as regarded text was the *Introduction to the Critical Study and Knowledge of the Holy Scriptures*, by Thomas Hartwell Horne, which passed through nine

Hahn,
Theile,
Bloomfield.

Horne's
" Introduction."

Tregelles's appreciation of Lachmann is very high, and his remarks concerning him are very interesting. Scrivener cannot accord to him the praise of wisdom in his design, or of overmuch industry and care in the execution of it; but styles him a true scholar, both in spirit and accomplishments, and ascribes to him the merit of restoring the Latin Versions to their proper rank in the criticism of the New Testament. Tischendorf, in his seventh edition, commented severely upon Lachmann's treatment of many passages, claiming that he had not followed his own principles. Dr. Gregory, in the Prolegomena to Tischendorf's eighth edition, speaks of him generously and discriminatingly.

[1] Dr. Gregory, Prolegomena to Tischendorf, 267, gives a list of manuscripts consulted by Bloomfield at Lambeth and in the British Museum, and Scrivener notices him only in an index of writers, owners, and collators. Tregelles (*Printed Text*, 262, note) says: " Those who maintain the traditional text often invent or dream their facts, and then draw their inferences. I refer the reader to Dr. Bloomfield's *Additional Annotations on the New Testament*, who, as well as other writers devoted to the advocacy of similar principles, habitually overlooks the real facts in the statement of evidence ; and thus he accuses critics of having made false allegations which really are not so, of inserting or cancelling readings which they have not inserted or cancelled, and of being actuated by evil motives, such as no one ought to think of imputing without sure knowledge and definite proof."

editions in England, from 1818 to 1846, and was printed three times in America, and commanded a wide influence.

Dœdes, Reiche, de Muralt.

In Holland, Jacob Isaac Dœdes, in 1844, published a *Treatise on the Textual Criticism of the New Testament,* in which he expressed the wish that the Textus Receptus might be set aside, and the text printed of an ancient manuscript, as A, with various readings from the oldest Greek codices. From George Reiche, Professor at Göttingen, came, in 1874, *A New Description* of some notable New Testament manuscripts in the Paris Library, and a collation with the Received Text.[1] The New Testament of Edward de Muralt, " ad fidem codicis principis Vaticani," Hamburg, 1848, was valuable principally for its collations of a few St. Petersburg codices. In England, John

Porter, Norton.

Scott Porter, a pupil of Griesbach and Hug, in his *Principles of Textual Criticism,* etc., 1848, and Samuel Davidson, in his *Treatise on Biblical Criticism,* 1852, gave some signs of a progress of the science. Good critical work in the history and text of the Gospels was done by Andrews Norton, Professor of Sacred Literature at Harvard Divinity School, in his *Evidences of the Genuineness of the Gospels,* 2d ed., 1846.

[1] Dr. Gregory characterises his work as "not unfruitful" with respect to certain minuscules, but says that he represents a backward tendency in criticism. Scrivener approvingly quotes Canon Cook's voucher for him as "a critic remarkable for extent and accuracy of learning, and for soundness and sobriety of judgment."

CHAPTER XIII

THE THIRD PERIOD (1830–81). TISCHENDORF

An important era in the history of Textual Criticism was marked by the labours of Ænotheus (Gottlob) Friedrich Constantine Tischendorf (1815–74). He was appointed Professor of Theology at Leipzig in 1843. In 1840 he began a series of journeys for the purpose of collecting and examining authorities for the New Testament text. From Paris, where he prepared for publication the text of Codex Ephraemi, he went to England, Holland, and Italy, examining and collating manuscripts in every great library. He was aided in his journeys by the pecuniary support of the Saxon and Russian governments. He aimed to become acquainted with all the uncial manuscripts by personal examination. His first journey to the East was made in 1844, when he discovered at the Mount Sinai Convent of St. Catherine forty-three leaves of Codex ℵ of the LXX, which had been thrown by the monks into a waste-basket to be used as fuel. These were published in 1846, as the Codex Friderico Augustanus. His third eastern excursion, in 1859, resulted in his discovery of the remainder of the Sinaitic Codex, including the entire New Testament. Having secured the loan of the codex, it was carried to Cairo, where, with the aid of two German scribes, he transcribed the whole manuscript of 110,000 lines, and noted the 12,000 changes made by later hands. In September, 1849, he was allowed to take it to Europe for publica-

Tischendorf. His series of journeys.

Discovery of Codex ℵ of LXX.

Discovery of ℵ of the New Testament.

Value of ℵ.

tion, and in 1862 it was issued in sumptuous style, in
four volumes, at the expense of Alexander II, Czar of
Russia. An edition containing only the New Testament appeared in the following year.[1] This discovery
was a most important contribution to the study of the
New Testament text. The date assigned by Tischendorf to the codex, the middle of the fourth century, is
generally accepted. He thought it probable that it
was one of the fifty copies which Constantine ordered
to be prepared for the churches of Constantinople in
331, and that it was sent by the Emperor Justinian to
the Sinaitic Convent which had been founded by him.
Tischendorf declared that a thousand readings of the
codex, among them exceedingly remarkable and important ones, sustained by the oldest Fathers and Versions, are found in neither B nor A. The readings, in
many passages, agree with those of B, and Tischendorf held that the hand of the same scribe was apparent in portions of both, though conceding that the
origin of the two was not the same. It contains twelve
thousand corrections, made by the original scribes or

---

[1] The story of the discovery of the Sinaitic Codex is told by
Tischendorf in *Reise in den Orient*, 1845–46, and most fully
in *Die Sinaibibel*, 1871. See also *Wann wurden unsere Evangelien verfasst ?* " When were our Gospels written ? " Translation by the London Religious Tract Society, 1867. Also
Georg Ebers, *Durch Gosen zum Sinai*, 302–309, Leipzig, 1872.
The charge that the manuscript was stolen under pretext of
borrowing is false. It was formally presented to the Czar in
1869 by the authorities of the Mt. Sinai Convent. Dr. Philip
Schaff says that Tischendorf, in 1871, showed him two letters
from Kallistratos the Prior, in one of which he distinctly says
that the codex was a gift ($\dot{\epsilon}\delta\omega\rho\dot{\eta}\theta\eta$) to the Russian emperor,
" as a testimony of eternal devotion." The Czar recognized the
gift by a liberal donation. See Schaff, *Companion to the Greek
Testament and English Version*, 3d ed., 111, and all the documentary evidence in Gregory's Prolegomena to Tischendorf,
350 f.

by later writers running from the fourth to the seventh century. It frequently agrees with the Old Latin.

The adherents of the Textus Receptus have endeavoured to belittle the importance and authority of this codex as well as that of B. Notable among these assailants was the late J. W. Burgon, Dean of Chichester, an accomplished scholar but a bitter controversialist. His views may be examined in *The Last Twelve Verses of the Gospel according to St. Mark Vindicated*, etc., London, 1871, and in *The Revision Revised*, London, 1883. His style of handling the two manuscripts may be seen from the following extracts, taken from the latter work: " By far the most depraved text is that exhibited by Codex D. . . . Next to D, the most untrustworthy codex is ℵ, which bears on its front a memorable note of the evil repute under which it has always laboured, viz. it is found that at least ten revisers between the fourth and the twelfth centuries busied themselves with the task of correcting its many and extraordinary perversions of the truth of Scripture. Next in impurity comes B." Referring to Bishop Ellicott's description of ℵ, B, A, and C, the Dean says : " Could ingenuity have devised severer satire than such a description of four professing *transcripts* of a book, and that book the everlasting Gospel itself ? . . . Imagine it gravely proposed, by the aid of four such conflicting documents, to readjust the text of the funeral oration of Pericles, or to reëdit *Hamlet. Risum teneatis amici ?* Why, some of the poet's most familiar lines would cease to be recognisable, *e.g.* A, — ' Toby or not Toby, that is the question ': B, — ' Toby or not, is the question ': ℵ, — ' To be a tub or not to be a tub, the question is that ': C, — ' The question is, to beat or not to beat Toby ? ' D (the ' singular codex '), — ' The only question is this, to beat that Toby or to be a tub ? ' "

Attempts to belittle its importance and authority. Burgon's attack.

"As for the origin of these two curiosities (ℵ and B), it can perforce only be divined from their contents. That they exhibit fabricated texts is demonstrable. No amount of honest copying — persevered in for any number of centuries — could by any possibility have resulted in two such documents. Separated from one another in actual date by fifty, perhaps by one hundred years, they must needs have branched off from a common corrupt ancestor, and straightway become exposed continuously to fresh depraving influences. The result is that Codex ℵ, which evidently has gone through more adventures and fallen into worse company than his rival, has been corrupted to a far graver extent than Codex B, and is even more untrustworthy."

"Lastly, we suspect that these two manuscripts are indebted for their preservation *solely to their ascertained evil character*, which has occasioned that the one eventually found its way, four centuries ago, to a forgotten shelf in the Vatican Library; while the other, after exercising the ingenuity of several generations of critical correctors, eventually got deposited in the waste-paper basket of the convent at the foot of Mt. Sinai. Had B and ℵ been copies of average purity, they must long since have shared the inevitable fate of books which are freely *used* and highly prized, namely, they would have fallen into decadence and disappeared from sight. But in the meantime, behold, their very antiquity has come to be reckoned to their advantage, and (strange to relate) is even considered to constitute a sufficient reason why they should enjoy not merely extraordinary consideration, but the actual surrender of the critical judgment."

Replies to Burgon.   Burgon was answered by Dr. Ezra Abbot of Cambridge, Mass., in the *Journal of the American Oriental Society,* 1872, X, 189–200, 602. Dr. Sanday, in the *Contemporary Review* for December, 1881, declared that the one thing which Burgon lacked was a grasp on the central condition of the problem, and that he did not seem to have the faintest glimmering of the principle of genealogy. He was also dealt with by O. von Gebhardt, in the article " Bibeltext " in Herzog's *Real-Encyklopädie.* In the same line with Burgon, but more moderate in tone, was Canon F. C. Cook, *The Revised Version of the First Three Gospels,* London, 1882.[1]

Tischendorf's labours as editor, writer, and collator were enormous. The catalogue of his published writings occupies fourteen pages of Gregory's Prolegomena. One of his principal claims to the gratitude of textual students is the number of texts of the leading uncials which he edited.[2] Between 1841 and 1873 he published twenty-four editions of the Greek Testament, if we include the reissues of his stereotyped *Editio Academica* (1855). Of these, four were intended rather for common or academic use than for critical purposes. The first edition of 1841 contained Prolegomena concerning Recensions, with special reference to the positions of Scholz, which he repudiated. In this edition he followed, essentially, the principles which he afterward maintained. In 1842 an edition was issued at Paris in large 8vo, with a Latin version according to ancient witnesses, and in the same year an edition in 12mo, without the version and the criti-

Tischen-dorf's editions of the New Testament.

---

[1] The most elaborate discussion of the Sinaitic and Vatican manuscripts is in Dr. Hort's Introduction to Westcott and Hort's *Greek Testament,* 210-270. See also F. H. A. Scrivener, *Collation of the Codex Sinaiticus,* 3d ed., 1867. Tischendorf, *Die Anfechtungen der Sinaibibel,* 1863. Id., *Waffen der Finsterniss wider die Sinaibibel,* 1863. Id., *Die Sinaibibel, ihre Entdeckung, Herausgabe und Erwerbung,* 1871. J. Rendel Harris, *New Testament Autographs,* Baltimore. V. Gardthausen, *Griechische Palaeographie,* 1879.

[2] See the list in Gregory's Prolegomena, 7 ff., and compare Scrivener's *Introduction,* II, 236 ff.

cal apparatus of the larger edition. Three editions
appeared in 1843, neither of which is specially sig-
nificant. His fifth or second Leipzig edition, 1849,
contained a revised text, with a selection of various
readings embodying the results of his own collations
since his first edition. "This edition may be called
epoch-making" (Bertheau). In this interval he had
copied or collated almost every known uncial. The
work also contained a statement of his critical principles. The seventh edition (*Editio Septima Critica
Major*, 1859) was issued in thirteen parts at Leipzig.
Scrivener characterises this as "a monument of per-
severing industry which the world has not often seen
surpassed." The Prolegomena, partly from the edition of 1849, were greatly enlarged. In the first
volume of this edition he showed a leaning toward
the Textus Receptus as represented by the cursives
and later uncials; but in the second volume he returned to the older uncial text. His crowning work,
the eighth edition (*Editio Octava Critica Major*), appeared in eleven parts, between 1864 and 1872. It
differed from that of 1859 in over three thousand
places, mostly in favour of the oldest uncial text.[1]

The eighth
larger
edition.

---

[1] Dr. Scrivener uses this fact to the disparagement of Tischendorf, remarking that it was "to the scandal of the science of
comparative criticism, as well as to his own grave discredit for
discernment and consistency." On the other hand, O. von Gebhardt, article "Bibeltext," Herzog's *Real-Encyklopädie*, regards
the fact as creditable to Tischendorf, showing his willingness to
learn from new sources of information. He says that the explanation lies not only in the enrichment of his textual apparatus
through the discovery of the Sinaitic Codex, but before all, as
Tischendorf himself declared, in the emphasis on the objective
authority of the oldest witnesses, irrespective of consequences
to subjective considerations, — those founded, for instance, on
possibilities of erroneous transcription, or the apparent critical
or dogmatic leanings of copyists.

Tischendorf's death in December, 1874, prevented the preparation of the Prolegomena to the eighth edition. This was done by Dr. Caspar René Gregory, assisted by Dr. Ezra Abbot, and was issued at Leipzig in 1894. Dr. Abbot died before the work was completed. "Cælestibus adjunctus animis," writes Dr. Gregory in his preface, "laude mea non eget." *The Prolegomena by Gregory and Abbot.*

Tischendorf started from Lachmann's principle, that the text is to be sought in ancient evidence, and especially in Greek manuscripts, but without neglecting the testimonies of Versions and Fathers. "I have learned," he said, "that the great profusion of various readings which is commonly paraded in books is a kind of splendid distress." Under the term, "most ancient Greek Codices," he included documents from the fourth to about the ninth century, classified according to their age, the older being the more authoritative. Their authority is strongly confirmed by the corroborating Versions and Fathers, and is not to be rejected, even though most or all of the modern copies read differently. His range was, accordingly, much larger than Lachmann's, and the application of his principle less rigid. While Lachmann aimed at attaining only the oldest text, Tischendorf sought for the best text. *Tischendorf's critical principles and methods.*

He treated the subject of recensions cautiously. He held that revisions were made by Hesychius and Lucian, but that the extent of the influence of these revisions could not be shown. The so-called revision of Origen existed, he declared, only in Hug's imagination. The documentary witnesses which have descended to us may be thrown into certain classes, especially in the Gospels, less in the Apocalypse than in the other books, more in the Pauline Epistles and Acts than in the Catholic Epistles. He recognised a fourfold division in two pairs: Alexandrian and Latin, *Classification of witnesses.*

Asiatic and Byzantine. The Alexandrian was in use among Eastern Jewish Christians, whose Greek, like that of the Apostles, was moulded by that of the Septuagint. The Latin was employed by Latins, whether Latin or Greek-speaking. The Asiatic prevailed among Greeks, whether in Asia or in their own country. The Byzantine was that which was diffused by the church throughout the Byzantine Empire, and which gradually, with the closer union of individual churches, acquired a kind of public unity. The Asiatic and Byzantine embraced the more recent documents; the Alexandrian and Latin the more ancient.

The question of the origin of these classes is not settled by the difference of the several countries through which the text was propagated, since the codices of one country were sometimes conveyed to another; as when Eusebius of Cæsarea and Athanasius of Alexandria were commanded by Constantine and Constans to send to the Byzantines copies accurately and elegantly transcribed. Along with the difference of countries there must be taken into the account the efforts made at a very early date to amend the text. Such efforts, Tischendorf thought, grew out of the want of reverence for "the written letter" on the part of the early Christians. It is to be especially observed that the Byzantine family is conspicuous in the great body of more recent Greek codices, and the Latin in the Latin and Græco-Latin documents, though with a great variety of readings. Of the Asiatic and Alexandrian the fewest documents survive, and none are uncorrupted. Great caution should therefore be exercised in applying the distinction of classes or recensions. To take this distinction as an absolute norm or foundation, is rash and futile. In assigning the first place to the Alexandrian witnesses we reason less from the theory of recensions than from the fact that

Caution demanded in applying the distinction of classes.

those codices which go under that name are almost the oldest of all surviving witnesses.

Thus, according to Tischendorf, the value of any codex is derived, not from its class, but from the goodness and antiquity of the text which the codex principally follows.[1]

Tischendorf laid down the following principles for the formation of his text, some of which had been, substantially, propounded by Griesbach and others:—

1. The text is only to be sought from ancient evidence, and especially from Greek manuscripts, but without neglecting the testimonies of Versions and Fathers. Thus the whole conformation of the text

Formal statement of Tischendorf's principles for the formation of his text.

---

[1] The uncial codices, arranged according to their value, are the following:—

(*A*) Text of the most ancient form, for the most part with an Alexandrian colouring, but with many variations.

(*B*) Text later in form, mostly with an Asiatic colouring.

Gospels

(*A*) Of the first rank: א A B C D I I^b L P Q R T^{a b c} X Z Δ (especially in Mark) Θ^{c g} Ξ.

Of the second rank: F^a N O W^{a b c} [W^{d e}] Y Θ^{a b e f} [Σ].

(*B*) Of the first rank, nearer to A: E K M Γ Λ Π Θ^h.

Of the second rank: F G H S U V.

When, as often occurs, E F G H K M S U V agree, they are designated by Tischendorf as unc⁹.

Acts and Catholic Epistles

(*A*) א A B C D I E G and P in Catholic Epistles, except in 1 Pet.

(*B*) H K L [M], and P in Acts and 1 Pet.

Pauline Epistles

(*A*) א A B C H I O Q [R] D F G M [O^b] P.

(*B*) K L N.

Apocalypse

(*A*) א A C P B.

should proceed from evidences themselves, and not
from what is called the *received* edition. The soundness of this rule, which embodies Lachmann's fundamental principle, is generally conceded. Its practical
working, however, strictly on Tischendorf's basis,
would be somewhat embarrassed by the wide range
which he gives to the term "Most Ancient Greek
Manuscripts"; since, under that term, he includes the
documents from the fourth to about the ninth century.
Later documents of that period would be likely to
exhibit readings resembling those of modern copies.
Tischendorf, however, declares that, of the documents
from the fourth to the ninth century, the authority of
the older ones is much the greater, and is confirmed by
corroborating testimonies of Versions and Fathers, and
not to be rejected, even though most or all of the
more modern copies read differently.

2. A reading altogether peculiar to one or another ancient document is suspicious, as also is any, even if supported by a class of documents which seems to show
that it has originated in the revision of a learned man.
He says that especially in the Gospels, where we have
several uncial manuscripts, it would be incautious to
receive a reading into the text on the authority of one
manuscript, unless the reading were in some measure
corroborated. On this Tregelles justly remarks that
"it seems unlikely that, in the Gospels, it would be
needful to rely on but one manuscript, unless, in such
a place, many of the leading authorities are defective, or unless the passage present a remarkable dis-
crepancy of reading. Tischendorf would apparently
introduce this latter limitation." An example is
furnished in Mark 2:22, where Tischendorf reads
ὁ οἶνος ἀπόλλυται καὶ οἱ ἀσκοί, "the wine perisheth and
the skins," for the received reading, ὁ οἶνος ἐκχεῖται καὶ
οἱ ἀσκοὶ ἀπολοῦνται, "the wine is spilled and the skins

perish." The former reading rests on the authority of B; but Tischendorf would refuse to adopt it on that authority alone. It is also the reading of the Memphitic Version, and added to these witnesses is the probability that it was altered in order to conform it to the reading of Matt. 9:17. That, originally, the passage in Mark was written differently from that in Matthew, in accordance with the difference between Matthew's fuller and Mark's briefer diction, would seem to be shown by the differences in reading of the passage in Mark. L reads ὁ οἶνος ἐκχεῖται καὶ οἱ ἀσκοὶ: D with It.ᵇ, ὁ οἶνος καὶ ἀσκοὶ ἀπολοῦνται. Thus, Tischendorf refuses to accept his reading on the authority of B alone, but accepts it because B is confirmed by a Version, and by the evidence of transcriptional probability.

3. Readings, however well supported by evidence, are to be rejected when it appears that they have proceeded from errors of copyists. Here, however, it is to be carefully considered whether an apparent transcriptional error is not set aside by the weight of diplomatic evidence. Thus, Tischendorf holds that the reading in Matt. 25:16 should be ἐποίησεν "made," instead of ἐκέρδησεν "gained"; but both Tregelles and Westcott and Hort retain ἐκέρδησεν on the ground that it is sustained by the best and most ancient manuscripts; and Tischendorf himself admits that it is often doubtful whether an apparent transcriptional error is really such. *Copyists' errors to be rejected despite support.*

4. In parallel passages, whether of the New or Old Testament, especially in the synoptical Gospels, those testimonies are to be preferred in which there is not precise accordance of such parallel passages, unless there are important reasons to the contrary. The tendency of copyists to bring the parallel passages of different Gospels into accord has already been noticed. *In parallel passages, unharmonised readings preferable.*

It was no doubt fostered by the use of Harmonies, such as Tatian's.

5. In discrepant readings, that reading should be preferred which may have given occasion to the rest, or which appears to comprise the elements of the others. The principle is sound, but its application is not easy in all cases, and is likely to depend upon the feeling of the individual critic. The same consideration will come into play as in Rule 3, viz. whether the apparent probability is not offset or overborne by external testimony.

6. Those readings must be maintained which accord with New Testament Greek, or with the peculiar style of each individual writer. This may be admitted so far as concerns the peculiar style of each writer; but the rule was evidently framed on the assumption that Biblical Greek was an independent language, an assumption which is strongly challenged by some modern New Testament scholars. Until that discussion is settled, it is premature to pronounce upon the validity of Tischendorf's rule.[1]

The question of the original New Testament text, and that of the methods by which it is to be finally determined, are both too far from absolute settlement to warrant a final judgment as to the relative value of Tischendorf's results. He himself incurred the charge of vacillation because he was open-eyed to all new forms of evidence, and ready to modify or to abandon former conclusions under the influence of new light.

[1] See H. A. A. Kennedy, *Sources of New Testament Greek*, Edinburgh, 1895. G. A. Deissmann, *Die sprachliche Erforschung der griechischen Bibel, ihr gegenwärtiger Stand und ihre Aufgaben*, Giessen, 1898. Id., *Beiträge zur Sprachgeschichte der griechischen Bibel*, in *Bibelstudien*, Marburg, 1895. Id., *Neue Bibelstudien. Sprachgeschichtliche Beiträge, zumeist aus den Papyri und Inschriften, zur Erklärung des Neuen Testaments*, Marburg, 1897.

The real value of Codex ℵ and his enthusiastic delight in its discovery may have led him sometimes to attach undue weight to its testimony.   In any case, he gave a vast and permanent impulse to the science of textual criticism, and advanced it far beyond the lines which it had previously reached.   He did not solve the problem presented by variations between the most ancient texts, but his accumulations of new manuscript evidence, from personal inspection, were enormous.   His collations were generally accurate, and his publications of the texts of the chief ancient witnesses were invaluable.   He was a formidable champion of the principle that the original text is to be determined primarily on the basis of ancient testimony.   Until some new and greater textual prophet shall arise, he will continue to divide the honors with Tregelles and Westcott and Hort, neither of whom have rendered his published results unnecessary ; and over a large area of the New Testament text the conclusions of these leaders coincide.[1]

---

[1] See Tischendorf, Prolegomena, 3–6, 7–22, 193–197.   Scrivener, *Introduction*, I, 115–117, 122, 155 f., 159, 163 ; II, 235–238, 282 ; also I, Index II.   P. Schaff, *Companion to the Greek Testament and English Version*, 3d ed., 103–111, 257–262. Tregelles, *Printed Text*, 116–129.   O. von Gebhardt, article "Bibeltext," in Herzog's *Real-Encyklopädie.*   J. E. Volbeding, *Constantine Tischendorf in seiner fünfundzwanzigjährigen schriftstellerischen Wirksamkeit*, Leipzig, 1862.   Ezra Abbot, *Unitarian Review*, March, 1875.   Carl Bertheau, article "Tischendorf," in Herzog's *Real-Encyklopädie.*

K

CHAPTER XIV

THIRD PERIOD (1830-81). TREGELLES

Tregelles's Prospectus.

SAMUEL PRIDEAUX TREGELLES, who ranks as one of the three great modern authorities on the New Testament text, was born and died at nearly the same times as Tischendorf. His *Prospectus of a Critical Edition of the Greek New Testament, now in preparation*, was appended to his *Book of Revelation Translated from the Ancient Greek Text*, 1844. In 1845 he went to Rome, with the special object of collating the Codex Vaticanus. This document had been already collated for Bentley by Mico (1799), partially by Birch, and also by Bartolocci (1669). Bartolocci's collation was not published. Tregelles had compared the two others, and had found that they differed in nearly two thousand places, and that many of the discrepancies were readings noticed by one and not by the other.

Fruitless attempt to collate B.

He went to Rome, and during the five months of his stay endeavoured to obtain permission to collate the manuscript accurately, or at least to examine it in the places where Birch and Bentley differed as to the readings; but all his efforts were in vain. He often saw the manuscript, but was hindered from transcribing any of its readings. He, however, read many passages, and afterward noted down several important readings.

During that visit, however, and two subsequent ones to the Continent, he examined all the manuscripts that he could find in different libraries, at Florence, Modena, Venice, Munich, Basle, Paris (where he transcribed Bartolocci's collation of B), Hamburg, Berlin, Leipzig,

130

and Dresden. In 1854 appeared his *Account of the Printed Text of the New Testament*, intended as an exposition of his critical principles; and in 1856 his *Introduction to the Textual Criticism of the New Testament*, contributed to the tenth edition of Horne's *Introduction*. In 1857 the first part of his Greek Testament, containing the Gospels of Matthew and Mark, was published, under the title, *The Greek Testament edited from Ancient Authorities, with the Latin Version of Jerome from the Codex Amiatinus.* The second part, containing the Gospels of Luke and John, followed in 1861, the Acts and Catholic Epistles appeared in 1865, and the Pauline Epistles, down to 2 Thessalonians, in 1869. He was disabled by a paralytic stroke in 1870; but the remaining Epistles were published in that year as he had prepared them. The Apocalypse, edited so far as possible, from his papers, by two of his friends, was issued in 1872, with a text differing in over two hundred places from his edition of 1844.

His New Testament contained a large array of Greek and Syriac readings, mostly the results of his own collations; besides readings of the Egyptian, Ethiopic, and Armenian Versions, of the Greek Fathers down to Eusebius, and of the Latin Fathers, Tertullian, Cyprian, Hilary, Lucifer of Cagliari, and Primasius. The Gospels were edited before the discovery of the Sinaitic Codex, and before Tischendorf's later studies on B. The lack of these two sources was the cause of many of his disagreements with Tischendorf's readings.[1]

Tregelles's collations of manuscripts were very extensive, and he devoted great attention to the Fathers.

[1] Gregory's Prolegomena to Tischendorf, 287–334, gives a collation of the texts of Tregelles and Westcott and Hort, with that of Tischendorf's eighth Critica Major.

Account of the Printed Text.

Introduction to the Textual Criticism of the New Testament.

His Greek Testament.

His critical work was distinguished by scrupulous exactness. Scrivener says that where Tischendorf and Tregelles differ in their collations, Tregelles is seldom in the wrong. In many cases he compared his own collations with Tischendorf's and settled the differences by a reëxamination of the manuscript.

Founder of "Comparative Criticism."

Tregelles introduced the method which he styled "Comparative Criticism," that is, the process which seeks to determine the comparative value and to trace the mutual relations of authorities of every kind upon which the original text of the New Testament is based. He ignored the Received Text and most of the cursives, and based his text on the oldest uncials, the Versions down to the seventh century, and the early Fathers. His range of ancient authorities was larger than Lachmann's. He denied that exactly defined families of documents could be distinguished, while admitting that two general classes of texts might be recognised, — Alexandrian and Constantinopolitan, — although some codices might occasionally be distinguished from the Alexandrian as " Western."

Critical principles.

His critical principles are stated at length in his "Printed Text." He lays down the following statements: Readings whose antiquity is proved apart from manuscripts are found in repeated instances in a few of the extant copies. These few, the text of which is thus proved to be ancient, include some, and often several, of the oldest manuscripts extant. In some cases the attested ancient reading is found in but one or two manuscripts, but those of the most ancient class. And, as certain manuscripts are found, by a process of inductive proof, to contain an ancient text, their character as witnesses must be considered to be so established that, in other places, their testimony deserves peculiar weight. As to Versions, the concurrence of two Versions in a definite reading excludes the supposition that the reading is merely an accident of transcription or translation; and that the accordance with them of certain manuscripts is likewise the result of fortuitous circumstances or of arbitrary alteration. When the number of according Versions is multiplied, the balance of probabilities is highly convincing. As to patristic citations, although often modernised to suit the Greek text to which a copyist was accustomed, yet when the reading is such that it could not be altered without changing the whole texture of their remarks, or when they are so express in their testimony that such a reading is that found in such a place, we need not doubt that it was so in their copies; and so, too, if we find that the reading of early Fathers agrees with other early testimonies in opposition to those which are later.

The antiquity of documents is to be preferred to their number as a basis of testimony. The only proof that a reading is ancient is that it is found in some ancient document. The selection of authorities must be based upon proof that the witnesses are worthy of confidence. Ancient manuscripts, the older Versions, and such early citations as have come down to us in a trustworthy form, are the only certain vouchers that any reading is ancient. Besides the manuscripts which are actually the oldest, we may use as valuable auxiliaries those whose general text accords with them, because the character of such manuscripts is shown by their general agreement with the oldest, and because it is also proved by the same criteria of accordance with the best early Versions and citations. It cannot be objected that we do not know by whom the ancient copies were written. This would apply equally to a vast number of the modern codices. The so-called uniform text of the later manuscripts is not an evidence in its favour, and does not show that the varia-

(marginal note) Insists on ancient testimony.

tions of the oldest manuscripts from one another and from the more recent prove the oldest to be unreliable. The later Greek manuscripts are not so uniform in their text as are the later Latin; yet the recent manuscripts of the Vulgate agree in perhaps two thousand readings, differing from what Jerome could have given, and also from the very few ancient copies which have been transmitted. Thus the Latin manuscripts supply an argument from analogy. The mass of recent copies contain a text notoriously and demonstrably incorrect; the few oldest manuscripts supply the means of emendation, and these few must be followed if we think of giving the genuine text of Jerome's Version. Besides all this, it is not strictly true that these more modern copies contain a uniform text. The difficulty of advocating the mass of modern copies is great, not only because of their internal variations, but also because the witnesses stand opposed to every one of the most ancient copies, to the ancient Versions as a class, and to every Christian writer of the first three centuries of whom we have any considerable remains.

Proposals in his New Testament. In his New Testament Tregelles proposes: (1) To give the text on the authority of the oldest manuscripts and Versions, and with the aid of the earlier citations, so as to present, as far as possible, the text commonly received in the fourth century, always stating what authorities support, and what oppose, the text given. (2) In cases in which we have certain proofs which carry us still nearer to the apostolic age, to use the data so afforded. (3) In cases in which the oldest documents agree in certain undoubted transcriptional error, to state the reading so supported, but not to follow it, and to give the grounds on which another reading is preferred. (4) In matters altogether doubtful, to state distinctly the conflicting evidence, and thus to approximate toward a true text. (5) To give the various readings of all the uncial manuscripts and ancient Versions very correctly, so that it may be clearly seen what readings possess any ancient authority whatever. To these add the more important citations of the earlier writers to Eusebius inclusive. The places are also to be indicated in which the common text departs from the ancient readings.

As compared with Tischendorf, Tregelles was more accurate in the use of his material, without being possessed of Tischendorf's resources. He was less restless than Tischendorf, and slower in making public the results of his labours, so that the different portions of his work do not exhibit the same changes of opinion which characterise Tischendorf. Both added immensely to the accumulations of evidence. *Tregelles and Tischendorf compared.*

In the inspection of Codex Basilianus in the Vatican (B of the Apocalypse), one of the three ancient copies which contain that book, he satisfied himself that the manuscript contained it entire, it having been previously supposed, owing to imperfect collation, that it had many gaps. At Florence, he collated the New Testament portion of the Codex Amiatinus, a most important manuscript of the Latin translation of Jerome, belonging to the sixth century. The previous partial collation by Fleck was defective and inaccurate. At Modena he made what was virtually the first collation of Codex Mutinensis of the Acts (ninth century). He was the first to collate Codex Nanii, V of the Gospels (tenth century), in the library of St. Mark at Venice. At Munich he collated Codex Monacensis, X of the Gospels (tenth century). This is an uncial manuscript with ancient readings, but with a commentary in cursive characters interspersed. Its collation was, in parts, exceedingly difficult, owing to the fading of the ink, and the difficulty was aggravated by Tregelles's bad eyes. The order of the Gospels is the reverse of *Tregelles's labours in collation.*

that in our Bibles, but before the beginning of John were two injured leaves, apparently overlooked by Tischendorf, and containing fragments of Matt. 6: 3–10. The important Codex Colbertinus, known as the Queen of the Cursives, and containing the Gospels, Acts, Catholic Epistles and Epistles of Paul, had been collated imperfectly by Larroque and Griesbach, and possibly by Scholz. It was reserved for Tregelles to do the work faithfully. He says, "I have had some experience in the collation of manuscripts, but none has ever been so wearisome to my eyes, and exhaustive of every faculty of attention, as this was." The leaves had been injured by damp, so that a part of the vellum was utterly destroyed. In the book of Acts the leaves were so firmly stuck together that, when they were separated, the ink adhered rather to the opposite page than to its own, so that, in many leaves, the manuscript could only be read by observing how the ink had *set off*, and thus reading the Greek words backward. He collated, in all, twenty-nine codices, besides editing Codex Zacynthius, Ξ, of Luke (eighth century), and O, a fragment of eight leaves (ninth century), containing about thirteen verses of the Gospel of John. The eight leaves of this manuscript were used for binding a copy of Chrysostom's Homilies which was brought from Mt. Athos to Moscow, where the leaves were discovered by Matthæi.

Von Gebhardt on Tischendorf and Tregelles.

Of Tischendorf and Tregelles, Dr. O. von Gebhardt says : "Both were in like measure equipped with the requisite qualities, — sharp-sightedness and an accuracy that gave heed to the smallest particulars, and both, with their whole soul, fixed their eyes upon the goal set before them, and strove with like zeal to reach it. That it was not their lot to attain equal success, lay in the fact that Tischendorf was much more enterprising, more keen-eyed for new discoveries, and far better favoured by fortune. But the success which each of them reached, at the same time, is so great that they leave far behind them everything that had been hitherto done in this realm. In the toilsome work of collating manuscripts and deciphering palimpsests, both Tischendorf and Tregelles spent many years of their lives, being thoroughly persuaded that the restoration of the New Testament text could be striven for with success only upon the basis of a diplomatically accurate investigation of the oldest documents. But while it was Tischendorf's peculiarity to publish in rapid succession the swiftly ripened fruits of his restless activity, and so to permit his last result to come into existence, so to speak, before the eyes of the public, Tregelles loved to fix his full energy undisturbed upon the attainment of the one great aim, and to come into publicity only with the completest which he had to offer. So we see Tischendorf editing the New Testament twenty times within the space of thirty years, not to mention his other numerous publications, while Tregelles did not believe that he could venture on the publication of the only edition of the New Testament which we possess from him, until after twenty years' preparation." [1]

Even Burgon, the bitter enemy of the principles of Tischendorf and Tregelles, says : "It is certain that by the conscientious diligence with which those distinguished scholars have respectively laboured, they have erected monuments of their learning and ability which will endure forever. Their editions of the New Testament will not be superseded by any new discoveries, by any future advances in the science of textual criticism. The manuscripts which they have edited will remain among the most precious materials for future study." [2]

Testimony of Burgon.

[1] Article "Bibeltext," in Herzog's *Real-Encyklopädie.*
[2] *The Last Twelve Verses of the Gospel according to St. Mark,*

Alford's
Greek
Testament.

Alford. — Henry Alford, Dean of Canterbury, issued the first volume of his Greek Testament in 1849. The fourth and final volume appeared in January, 1861. The several volumes passed through numerous editions. Seven of the first two volumes, and five of the third and fourth, were published. In the fifth edition he nearly rewrote the text and digest of readings, chiefly on the basis of the labours of Tischendorf and Tregelles. In the sixth he incorporated the readings of the Codex Sinaiticus. He added another protest against the irrational reverence for the Textus Receptus as standing in the way of all chance of discovering "the genuine word of God," and advocated a return to the evidence of the most ancient witnesses as against the imposing array of later manuscripts. He says : "Experience has brought about some changes in my convictions with regard to the application of canons of subjective criticism to the consensus of ancient manuscripts. In proportion as I have been led severely to examine how far we can safely depend on such subjective considerations, I confess that the limits of their applicability have become narrowed. In very many cases they may be made to tell with equal force either way." He drew his apparatus mostly from the works of others, but himself compared B in selected passages, and contributed some new readings from other sources. His text appears to be nearer to that of Tregelles than to that of Tischendorf.

Protests
against rev-
erence for
the Textus
Receptus.

Preface, viii, ix. See Tischendorf, Prolegomena, 269–272. Tregelles, *Account of the Printed Text of the Greek New Testament.* Carl Bertheau, article "Tregelles," in Herzog's *Real-Encyklopädie.* O. von Gebhardt, article " Bibeltext," in Herzog's *Real-Encyklopädie.* Scrivener, *Introduction,* II, 238–241. F. J. A. Hort, *Journal of Philology,* March, 1858. T. H. Horne, *Introduction to the Critical Study and Knowledge of the Holy Scriptures,* 10th ed., IV, 1856 ; 11th ed., 1863.

CHAPTER XV

THIRD PERIOD (1830–81). REACTION TOWARD THE
TEXTUS RECEPTUS. SCRIVENER AND BURGON

UNDER the influence of Tregelles, many English
scholars returned to the principles of Bentley. Dr.
Gregory naïvely remarks, at this point, "Non tamen
desunt viri docti quibus hæc novitas vix placeat."
Tregelles himself feelingly alludes to this. "It is
to be lamented that the feeling thus exists, even on
the part of some scholars, that recurrence to the most
ancient sources for the text of Scripture deserves to be
so condemned and deprecated that they hold up critics
(conscientious men it may be) who press the importance of ancient testimony, as reckless innovators, and
they thus lead an unjudging crowd to condemn them
and their labours." Tregelles found himself in conflict
with the leading representative of the conservative
school of Textual Criticism in England, Dr. Frederick
Henry Ambrose Scrivener, Prebendary of Exeter and
Vicar of Hendon. Dr. Scrivener's attitude is set forth
in his own words in the second edition of his *Introduction*, repeated in the fourth and last edition.
"All that can be inferred from searching into the
history of the sacred text amounts to no more than
this: that extensive variations, arising no doubt from
the wide circulation of the New Testament in different
regions and among nations of diverse languages, sub-
sisted from the earliest period to which our records
extend. Beyond this point our investigations cannot

Dr. Scrive-
ner. leader
of the con-
servative
textualists
in England.

be carried without indulging in pleasant speculations, which may amuse the fancy but cannot inform the sober judgment."

Works by Scrivener. Dr. Scrivener, in 1860, edited Stephen's text of 1550, adding the readings of the Elzevirs, Beza, Lachmann, Tischendorf, and Tregelles. Six editions are noted by Dr. Gregory, the latest in 1877. In 1881 appeared *The New Testament in the Original Greek according to the Text followed in the Authorised Version (T. R. Beza, 1598), together with the Variations adopted in the Revised Version.* An appendix gives a list of the passages in which the Authorised Version departs from Beza's text and agrees with certain earlier editions of the Greek Testament. An important contribution to the study of Textual Criticism was his *Plain Introduction to the Criticism of the New Testament,* 1861. The fourth edition, revised, and enlarged to two volumes, appeared in 1894, edited by the Rev. Edward Miller, an earnest supporter of the conservative school. The list of manuscripts has been increased to 3791, and most of the accounts of ancient Versions have been rewritten by eminent specialists. Notwithstanding its extremely conservative character, the work is valuable. Dr. Scrivener was possessed of large learning on textual questions, but fought every inch of the ground yielded by the Received Text. His experience led him gradually to modify his views on some points, and to make some concessions. At the time of his death he was moving in the direction of the substitution of the older, uncial text for that of the Textus Receptus. He gave up 1 John 5:7, 8, and decided for ὅς against θεὸς in 1 Timothy 3:16. The movement, however, was slow and hesitating. In his last edition of Stephen's text (1887) he characterised Westcott and Hort's edition as "splendidum peccatum, non κτῆμα ἐς ἀεί."

With Dean Burgon he stood for the position that
all available authorities, and not the most ancient
only, should be considered in the settlement of the
text, and earnestly combated the tendency to rely too
exclusively on the testimony of ℵ and B. He was,
however, more moderate than Burgon, who pronounced
ℵ and B to be the most corrupt of manuscripts.
Scrivener says: "We accord to Codex B at least as
much weight as to any single document in existence;"
and again, "We have no wish to dissemble the great
value of the Codex Vaticanus, which, in common with
our opponents, we regard as the most weighty single
authority that we possess." He also differed with
Burgon on 1 Tim. 3 : 16. In the last edition of the
Introduction his discussion of principles is summed
up in four practical rules: (1) That the true readings
of the Greek New Testament cannot safely be derived
from any one set of authorities, whether manuscripts,
Versions, or Fathers, but ought to be the result of a
patient comparison and careful estimate of the evidence supplied by them all.   (2) That where there is
a real agreement between all documents containing the
Gospels up to the sixth century, and in the other parts
of the New Testament up to the ninth, the testimony
of later manuscripts and Versions, though not to be
rejected unheard, must be regarded with great suspicion, and unless upheld by strong internal evidence,
can hardly be adopted.   (3) That where the more
ancient documents are at variance with each other,
the later uncial and cursive copies, especially those of
approved merit, are of real importance as being the
surviving representatives of other codices, very probably as early, perhaps even earlier, than any now
extant.   (4) That in weighing conflicting evidence we
must assign the highest value, not to those readings
which are attested by the greatest number of wit-

*Opinion of
Codex B.*

*Critical
principles
summed up.*

nesses, but to those which come to us from several remote and independent sources, and which bear the least likeness to each other in respect to genius and general character.

He admits that the principle of grouping is sound, but with certain reservations. A full statement of his opinions on the late views of comparative criticism is given in the *Introduction*, II, X.

Burgon's defence of Mark 16 : 9–20.

Burgon. — John W. Burgon, Dean of Chichester, was the friend and coadjutor of Scrivener. He is known principally by his elaborate defence of the authenticity of the last twelve verses of Mark's Gospel, and by his savage attack on the Revised Version. He was a learned scholar and an acute critic, and did much work in inspecting and collating manuscripts, especially cursives, in France and Italy. Much of his work was published in *The Guardian,* and is not easily accessible. "Burgon's work is dominated by the conviction that every word of the Scriptures was dictated by the inspiration of the Holy Spirit; that it is inconceivable that the Author of such a gift would allow it to become unavailing, and would not providentially interfere to guard it from being corrupted or lost; that we may therefore rightly believe that He guided His church through the course of ages to eliminate the errors which the frailty of man had introduced, and conse-

His textual principles.

quently that the text which has been used by the church for centuries must be accepted as at least substantially correct." [1] Testing the value of the ancient manuscripts by comparison with the Textus Receptus, he stated his conclusion as follows: " By far the most depraved text is that exhibited by Codex D; next to D the most untrustworthy codex is ℵ; next in impurity comes B; then the fragmentary Codex C; our own

[1] Dr. Salmon, *Some Thoughts on the Textual Criticism of the New Testament.*

A being beyond all doubt disfigured by the fewest blemishes of any." According to Burgon, the antiquity of the most ancient manuscripts is due to their badness. They were known to be so bad that they were little used, and consequently remained untouched, and therefore have survived when better manuscripts have perished.[1]

Green, Kelly, McClellan, Abbot, Ward, Tyler. — Thomas Sheldon Green, of Cambridge, is known by *A Course of Developed Criticism on Passages of the New Testament, materially affected by Various Readings*, London, 1856 ; *The Twofold New Testament, being a New Translation accompanying a newly formed Text*, London, 1865 ; *A Critical Appendix to the Twofold New Testament*, London, 1871. His text was based on ancient witnesses, and agreed, mainly, with Tregelles and Tischendorf. The text of the Apocalypse was edited by William Kelly, *The Revelation of John edited in Greek with a New English Version and a Statement of the Chief Authorities and Various Readings*, London, 1860. John Brown McClellan published *The New Testament . . . a New Translation . . . from a critically revised Greek Text . . . Harmony of the Four Gospels, Notes, and Dissertations.* Only the first volume, containing the Four Gospels, appeared (London, 1875). Like Burgon, he condemned ℵ and B as the worst codices, and regarded internal probability as the surest guide in distinguishing between disputed readings.

The lamented Ezra Abbot, from the year 1856, devoted himself to the New Testament text, though he made no attempt to edit a text. The results of his studies appeared in numerous articles and pamphlets, a list of which may be found in Gregory's Prolegomena,

Thomas Sheldon Green.

William Kelly and John B. McClellan.

Ezra Abbot.

[1] Many interesting particulars concerning Burgon will be found in Dr. Schaff's *Companion to the Greek Testament and English Version*, 3d ed., 84, 108, 119 ff., 191, 293 ff., 378, 425, 491.

276.   Also in the volume *Anglo-American Bible Revision*, New York, 1879, 86–98, in *The New Revision and its Study*, Philadelphia, 1881, reprinted in part in B. H. Kennedy's *Ely Lectures on the Revised Version of the New Testament*, London, 1882, and in the American edition of Smith's *Dictionary of the Bible*, 1866–70. He was one of the American committee on the Revised Version, and was associated with Dr. C. R. Gregory in the preparation of the Prolegomena of Tischendorf's eighth edition.   Mention should also be made of the W. H. Ward, treatise of Dr. William Hayes Ward of New York, A. W. Tyler. *Examination of the Various Readings of* 1 *Timothy* 3 : 16, Bibliotheca Sacra, Andover, 1865, and of two Dissertations by A. Wellington Tyler, *Our Lord's Sacerdotal Prayer, John* 17, *a New Critical Text*, etc., and *Paul's Panegyric of Love, a New Critical Text*, etc., Bibliotheca Sacra, 1871, 1873; also a Critical Apparatus to 1 Cor. 12 : 27 — 13 : 13, in which the Patristic witnesses are carefully collected.

CHAPTER XVI

THIRD PERIOD (1830-81). WESTCOTT AND HORT, AND THE REVISERS' TEXT OF 1881

IN 1881 appeared *The New Testament in the Original Greek*, two volumes, Cambridge and London, by Brooke Foss Westcott, D.D., Canon of Peterborough and Regius Professor of Divinity at Cambridge, and now Bishop of Durham, and Fenton John Anthony Hort, D.D., Hulsean Professor of Divinity at Cambridge. The first volume contained the text, and the second the exposition of the textual principles and methods of the editors, with notes on select readings, orthography, and Old Testament quotations. *Westcott and Hort's New Testament.*

This work was announced as an attempt to present exactly the original words of the New Testament, so far as they can now be determined from surviving documents, by the application of criticism in distinguishing and setting aside those readings which have originated at some link in the chain of transmission. The editors made no attempt to amass new material, but chose to rely upon the stores accumulated by their predecessors, confining themselves to the work of investigating and editing the text itself. Their fresh evidence was chiefly patristic, derived in a great measure from writings or fragments of writings first published during the last hundred years, or now edited from better manuscripts than were formerly known.

Their textual principles were elaborated in their Introduction, prepared by Dr. Hort, a technical work *The Introduction.*

of enormous labour. To this the reader must be referred, since it is impossible adequately to exhibit its contents in a condensed statement.

The aim, then, of Westcott and Hort, like that of Tischendorf and Tregelles, is to make the closest approximation to the apostolic text itself, thus placing their objective point back of Lachmann's, which was the text of the fourth century. The facts of textual history, they assert, as attested by Versions and patristic quotations, show that it is no longer possible to speak of "the text of the fourth century," since most of the important variations were in existence before the middle of the fourth century, and many can be traced back to the second. "Thus the text of this edition, in that larger sense of the word 'text' which includes the margin, rests exclusively on direct ancient authority, and its primary text rests exclusively on direct ancient authority of the highest kind."

Text claims to be based on the highest ancient authority.

The proper method of textual genealogy consists in the more or less complete recovery of the texts of successive ancestors by analysis and comparison of the varying texts of their respective descendants, each ancestral text so recovered being in its turn used, in conjunction with other similar texts, for the recovery of a text of a yet earlier common ancestor.

The object, in brief, is, instead of simply estimating authorities in the order of their age, to arrange them into groups which have descended from common ancestors, and determine the age and character of each group. All the documents representing a text are examined with a view to tracing out the resemblances between them, and so classifying them in groups, larger or smaller, according to likeness. This process grows out of the principle that identity of reading implies identity of origin. Though it is possible that identity of reading may arise from accidental coin-

Genealogical method.

cidence, yet the chances in favour of that possibility
are relatively small, and diminish with the increase of
the number of texts which agree in the reading. The
great bulk of identities of reading may be taken as
certain evidence of a common origin. In other words,
classification of documents according to their resemblance is a classification of them according to origin.
This community of origin may be either complete,
that is, due to a common ancestry for their whole
texts, or partial, that is, due to mixture.

This factor of mixture greatly complicates the process. If each document were derived simply from a
single previous document, all the documents, each with
its single parent, would fall into a simple genealogy.
But a text may be mixed, that is, it may not have
been copied from a single exemplar, but from two or
more of different types, the copyist selecting the reading now of one and now of another, or combining the
readings by mere addition, or by fusing them, thus
making what are termed "conflate" readings. Or
again, a copyist might have been familiar with a document of a different type from that from which he was
copying, and might have introduced its readings, from
memory, into his own copy. Or he might have introduced into the text of his copy corrections from other
codices which he found in the margin of his exemplar.
The result would be a mixed text, which would confuse genealogy.

Dr. Hort distinguishes four types of text in the surviving documents: 1. Western. This appears to have
originated in Syria or Asia Minor, and to have been
carried thence to Rome and Africa, and also to have
passed through Palestine and Egypt into Ethiopia. It
is represented especially by D (Gospels and Acts), and
D$_2$ (Pauline Epistles), the Old Latin Versions, and the
Greek copies on which they were based, and, in part,

*"Conflate"
readings.*

*Types of
text:
1. Western.*

by the Curetonian Syriac. It appears to have been most widely diffused in Ante-Nicene times, and is the text of the Ante-Nicene Fathers who were not connected with Alexandria,—Justin, Irenæus, Hippolytus, Methodius. It is an independent text, quite distinct from all other types. Its prevailing characteristic is a love of paraphrase and of interpolation with a view to enrich the text. It is marked by additions, omissions, and assimilations of parallel passages. These peculiarities go to show that it originated at a time when little regard was paid to the exact words of the apostolic writings as compared with their substance; probably before the end of the second century.

2. Alexandrian. 2. Alexandrian or Egyptian. This seems to have proceeded from a learned and skilful hand in the beginning of the third century, or even earlier. It is found in the quotations of the Alexandrian Fathers — Clement, Origen, Dionysius, Didymus, Cyril — and in the Egyptian Versions, especially the Memphitic. It also appears, in part, in Eusebius of Cæsarea. Its characteristic is that which might be expected from the influence of a Greek literary centre — a tendency to polish the language by correcting forms, syntax, etc.

3. Syrian. 3. Syrian. This was a mixed text, the result of a recension or revision of editors who desired to present the New Testament in a smooth and attractive form, and accordingly borrowed from all sources. It is best represented by A (in the Gospels, not in the Acts and Epistles), and by the Peshitto as distinct from the Curetonian. Its readings are found in the Scripture quotations of Chrysostom, who was Bishop of Syrian Antioch until 398, and Patriarch of Constantinople until his death in 407; also in those of Theodore of Mopsuestia (*ob.* 429), and of Diodorus of Antioch and Tarsus. The group is therefore also called Antiochian. Generally speaking, these readings are common in the

Fathers of the latter part of the fourth century and in all subsequent Fathers, but cannot be traced in the quotations of the Ante-Nicene Fathers. "The favourite text of Chrysostom and his age has disappeared entirely from use by the time we reach Origen" (Warfield). The text is that of the mass of the cursives, most of which were written in Constantinople, and is mainly identical with the printed Textus Receptus. It is an eclectic text, marked by conflate readings, the elements of which are found in the other classes, and indicates an attempt to harmonise at least three conflicting texts. It contains no ancient element that is not in these.

"The qualities which the authors of the Syrian text seem to have most desired to impress on it are lucidity and completeness. They were evidently anxious to remove all stumbling-blocks out of the way of the ordinary reader, so far as this could be done without recourse to violent measures. They were apparently equally desirous that he should have the benefit of instructive matter contained in all the existing texts, provided it did not confuse the context or introduce seeming contradictions. New omissions, accordingly, are rare, and where they occur are usually found to contribute to apparent simplicity. New interpolations, on the other hand, are abundant, most of them being due to harmonistic or other assimilation, fortunately capricious and incomplete. Both in matter and in diction the Syrian text is conspicuously a full text. It delights in pronouns, conjunctions, and expletives, and supplied links of all kinds, as well as in more considerable additions. As distinguished from the bold vigour of the Western scribes, and the refined scholarship of the Alexandrians, the spirit of its own corrections is at once sensible and feeble. Entirely blameless on either literary or religious grounds as

Qualities of the Syrian text.

regards vulgarised or unworthy diction, yet showing no marks of either critical or spiritual insight, it presents the New Testament in a form smooth and attractive, but appreciably impoverished in sense and force, more fitted for cursory perusal or recitation than for repeated and diligent study." [1] Syrian readings, being later than Western and Alexandrian, and derived from Western and older sources, are to be rejected when their testimony differs from that of the others.

4. Neutral or pre-Syrian. 4. Neutral or pre-Syrian. This is represented by B and largely by ℵ, and comes nearest to the Apostolic originals. It cannot be assigned to any local centre, but belongs originally to all the Eastern world. It is characterised by careful copying, and is free from Western corruptions. It appears in places far removed from Alexandria. In Asia Minor it was superseded by the Western text. The common original of B and ℵ, for by far the greater part of their identical readings, whatever may have been its own date, has a very ancient and pure text. Their coincidences are due to the extreme antiquity of the common original from which the ancestors of the two manuscripts have diverged, the date of which cannot be later than the early part of the second century, and may well be yet earlier. There is no clear difference of character in the fundamental text common to B and ℵ in any part of the New Testament in which B is not defective. The textual phenomena which we find when we compare them singly and jointly with other documents are, throughout, precisely those which would present themselves in representatives of two single lines diverging from a point near the autographs, and not coming into contact subsequently.

The readings of the Neutral text, when established,

---

[1] Dr. Hort, Introduction, § 187.

are to be accepted in the face of the numerical preponderance of other texts.

Dr. Hort thus recapitulates: "The continuity, it will be seen, is complete. Early in the second century we find the Western text already wandering into greater and greater adulteration of the Apostolic text, which, while doubtless holding its ground in different places, has its securest refuge at Alexandria; but there, in turn, it suffers from another but slighter series of changes, and all this before the middle of the third century. At no long time after, we find an attempt made, apparently at Antioch, to remedy the growing confusion of texts by the editing of an eclectic text combining readings from the three principal texts, itself further revised on like principles, and in that form used by great Antiochian theologians not long after the middle of the fourth century. From that date, and indeed earlier, we find a chaos of varying mixed texts, in which, as time advances, the elder texts recede, and the Antiochian text, now established at Constantinople, increasingly prevails. Then even the later types with mixed base disappear, and, with the rarest exceptions, the Constantinopolitan text alone is copied, often at first with relics of its vanquished rivals included, till at last these two dwindle, and in the copies written shortly before the invention of printing, its victory is all but complete. At each stage there are irregularities and obscurities; but we believe the above to be a true sketch of the leading incidents in the history of the text of the New Testament; and, if it be true, its significance as a key to the complexities of documentary evidence is patent without explanation."

Dr. Hort recapitulates.

Briefly, then, while the majority of our extant manuscripts contain a revised, and therefore less original, text, a comparatively small group contains texts which were not subject to this revision or were prior to it. Consequently, the evidence of this small group is usually to be preferred to that of the great mass of manuscripts and versions.

Reception of Westcott and Hort's Testament. Westcott and Hort's New Testament received a cordial welcome from many scholars in England and elsewhere, from Roman Catholics as well as Protestants.[1] On the other hand, the work was severely attacked by the conservative critics, notably by Dr. Scrivener and Dean Burgon.

Points assailed. Perhaps the most vulnerable point was the very corner-stone of the textual theory — the authoritative recension at Antioch of the Greek text,

The third-century recension. about the middle of the third century, which, in its turn, became the standard for a similar revision of the Syrian text, representing the transmutation of the Curetonian into the Peshitto, while the Greek recension itself underwent a second revision.[2] Dr. Scrivener says: "Of this twofold authoritative revision of the Greek text, of this formal transmutation of the Curetonian Syriac into the Peshitto, although they must have been, of necessity, public acts of great churches in ages abounding in councils, general or provincial, not one trace remains in the history of Christian antiquity; no one writer seems conscious that any modification, either of the Greek Scriptures or of the vernacular translation, was made in or before his time. It is as if the Bishops' Bible had been thrust out of the English Church service and out of the studies of her divines, and the Bible of 1611 had silently taken its place, no one knew how, or when, or why, or, indeed, that any change whatever had been made. Yet, regarding his speculative conjecture as indubitably true,

---

[1] Dr. Schaff has collected a number of tributes in his *Companion to the Greek Testament and English Version*, 3d ed., 280 ff.

[2] See Hort's Introduction, §§ 189, 190.

Dr. Hort proceeds to name the text as it stood before his imaginary era of transfusion, a pre-Syrian text, and that into which it was changed, sometimes Antiochian, more often Syrian; while of the latter recension, though made deliberately, as our author believes, by the authoritative voice of the Eastern Church, he does not shrink from declaring that all distinctively Syrian readings must be at once rejected, thus making a clean sweep of all critical materials, — Fathers, Versions, manuscripts, uncial or cursive, comprising about nineteen-twentieths of the whole mass, which do not correspond with his preconceived opinion of what a correct text ought to be."

Exception was also taken to the editors' omissions from the text; to their inconsistency in rejecting Western readings on the one hand, and on the other in indorsing their omissions of what was attested by other authorities. The names given to the families of texts were challenged. The term "Western" was declared to be inaccurate, since the type of text so designated was not confined to the West, and even the editors admit that readings of this class were current in the East as well as in the West, and probably, to a great extent, had originated there. The name "Neutral" was condemned, as presupposing that all additions or alterations in the text were due to later corruptions. Also the name "Alexandrian," because used in a sense not previously employed. It was further objected that the designation of the Curetonian Syriac as "the Old Syriac," and of the Peshitto as "the Vulgate," begged the whole question of the relative age of the two. The editors were severely taken to task for assigning undue weight to the testimony of ℵ and B. "That ℵ B should thus lift up their heads against all the world is much, especially having regard to the fact that several Versions and not a few Fathers are older than they; for

[marginal notes:] Omissions. Names given to families of texts.

Designation of Curetonian as "Old Syriac." Undue weight assigned to ℵ and B.

while we grant that a simple patristic citation, standing by itself, is of little value, yet when the context or current of exposition renders it clear what reading these writers had before them, they must surely, for that passage, be equivalent as authorities to a manuscript of their own age " (Scrivener).[1]

Revisers of 1881 did not construct a Greek text. **The Revisers of 1881.** — The history of the Revised Version of 1881 is too well known to require recapitulation. Naturally a large proportion of the changes introduced by the Revisers grew out of differences in the text translated. The Revisers, in the matter of text, did not claim to be discoverers. They confined themselves mostly to the verification and registration of the best-established conclusions of modern textual criticism. Their text was drawn from the best documentary sources which have been discovered in the last three hundred years. It has been estimated that the Greek text of 1881 differs from that of 1611 in at least 5788 readings. In their preface the Revisers say, " A revision of the Greek text was the necessary foundation of our work, but it did not fall within our province to construct a continuous and complete Greek text."

In the English committee, Dr. Hort and Dr. Scrivener were the recognised authorities on textual questions. The traditional text and the later text had therefore each a fair hearing. The Revisers followed the text of Westcott and Hort closely, though not absolutely. "The combination of ℵ B with two or more of the

---

[1] The principal objections are well stated in the recent volume of Dr. George Salmon, Provost of Trinity College, Dublin : *Some Thoughts on the Textual Criticism of the New Testament*, London, 1897. The book has a peculiar interest as coming from a close personal friend of Dr. Hort. The textual theory of the two editors is handled with great candour and discrimination, and some of the points against it are very effectively made.

greater uncials has been treated by them as all but de- cisive. The combination of אַ B with one other first-class uncial has also had the greatest weight. There are forty-one instances of agreement with this combination, and only three instances of difference from it. In the case of the single pair אַ B alone, there is much greater indecision. Their authority has been followed in from fifteen to nineteen cases, and rejected in twelve. With any other single supporter than אַ, B has carried less weight still, the numbers here being eleven to four, while the isolated evidence of B has been rejected in nine out of ten cases " (Professor Sanday).[1]

Two editions of the Greek Testament, which have a special interest in connection with the Revised Version, appeared simultaneously with the edition of Westcott and Hort. The Revisers were not, however, responsible for their publication. Neither claimed to be an independent, critical recension of the text. The first was by Dr. Scrivener, *The New Testament in the Original* *Greek according to the Text followed in the Authorised Version, together with the Variations adopted in the Revised Version*, Cambridge, 1881. The new readings were placed at the foot of the page, and the displaced readings were printed in the text in heavier type. The appendix furnished a list of the passages in which the Authorised Version differs from Beza's text of 1598, and agrees with certain earlier editions of the Greek Testament. The other edition was by Dr. E. Palmer, Archdeacon of Oxford, Η ΚΑΙΝΗ ΔΙΑΘΗΚΗ. *The Greek Testament with the Readings adopted by the Re-*

---

[1] On the Revisers' text see a series of articles by Rev. W. Sanday, D.D., *The Revised Version of the New Testament*, in the Expositor, 2d series, II, 1881 ; very valuable. See also Dr. B. B. Warfield, *Presbyterian Quarterly*, April, 1882, and *The Revisers and the Greek Text of the New Testament*, London, 1882, supposed to be by Bishop Ellicott and Archdeacon Palmer.

visers of the Authorised Version, Oxford, 1881. Palmer
gave the Greek text followed by the Revisers, and
placed the rejected readings of the Textus Receptus
and of the Authorised Version in foot-notes. The continuous text has for its basis Stephen's third edition
(1550), which is followed in all cases where the Revisers do not prefer other readings. Stephen's orthography, spelling of proper names, and typographical
peculiarities or errors are, with a few exceptions, retained, together with his marking of chapters. The
verses are distributed according to the Authorised Version.

CHAPTER XVII

RECENT CONTRIBUTIONS. WEISS. STUDIES IN CODEX D

DR. BERNHARD WEISS of Berlin has, for some time, been carrying on a new and independent construction of the text. No summary statement of his textual principles has been presented, so far as I am aware, either by himself or by others. The results of his work appear in minute detail in his *Neue Testament. Textkritische Untersuchungen und Textherstellung.* Vol. I, Leipzig, 1893, contains the Acts, Catholic Epistles, and Apocalypse; Vol. II, 1896, the Pauline Epistles. He complains that he has been constantly annoyed in his exegetical work by the uncertainty of the text. Neither the usual reasons of the commentators for determining the value of various readings nor the modern editions of the text appeared to offer him a satisfactory and certain path toward a decision. The collations in Tischendorf's apparatus need to be verified anew. He treats the text under the heads of Omissions and Additions, Changes of Position, and Orthographical Variations.[1]

Studies in the Codex Bezæ. — Within a few years special attention has been directed at the peculiar readings of the Codex Bezæ (D, Gospels and Acts) and their bearing upon the history of the text. The following section on this subject has been prepared by the Rev. James Everett Frame, Instructor in the New

(margin: Dr. Weiss's construction of the text.)

(margin: Rev. J. E. Frame on Codex Bezæ.)

[1] See C. R. Gregory, "Bernhard Weiss and the New Testament," *American Journal of Theology*, January, 1897.

Testament Department of Union Theological Seminary, New York.

"When every allowance has been made for possible individual license, the text of D presents a truer image of the form in which the Gospels and Acts were most widely read in the third and probably a great part of the second century, than any other extant Greek manuscript." So Dr. Hort (Introduction, 2d ed., 149). Codex Bezæ, along with the Sinaiticus and the Vaticanus, exhibits "the most shamefully mutilated text," and has become the depository of "the largest amount of fabricated readings, ancient blunders, and intentional perversions of truth which are discernible in any known copies of the Word of God." So Dean Burgon (*Revision Revised*, 16). These opinions have been registered to indicate at the outset the diversity of views which prevail in regard to this puzzling uncial.

Codex Bezæ is a bilingual, Greek and Latin, so arranged that the Greek text has the place of honour on the left side of the open book, while the Latin Version has the right side. It contains at present the Gospels and Acts, though not a few leaves are missing, as, for instance, Acts 22 : 29–28 : 31, which is lacking in both D (the Greek text) and d (the Latin Version). It is divided into lines or verses, that is, the arrangement is stichometric, although the divisions into lines do not always correspond with the divisions in sense. As to date, it is generally assigned to the beginning of the sixth century. It was first brought to public notice ten centuries later by Beza, who got possession of it in 1562. How long it had lain in the Monastery of Irenæus in Lyons, whence Beza obtained it, is uncertain. In 1581 Beza presented it to the University of Cambridge, that it might be preserved, but not published; for he thought the vari-

[margin note:] Contradictory views of Hort and Burgon.

[margin note:] History of Codex Bezæ.

PLATE VII

SPECIMEN HALF-PAGES OF THE CODEX BEZAE, CAMBRIDGE

(Original size of pages 7½ in. × 10 in., including the margins, which in the reproduction have been slightly trimmed to avoid further reduction in size of the text.)

ants, especially in Luke, might give offence. The warning was heeded, although Beza himself had published some of the variants in his Greek Testament, and other readings became known. Finally, however, William Whiston, the translator of Josephus, did the Codex into English in 1747; and in 1793 Thomas Kipling published the first edition of the Codex, calling it, after the name of its donor and of the University to which it was given, *The Cambridge Codex of Theodore Beza.*[1] *First published edition of Codex Bezæ.*

An accurate edition, "being an exact copy in ordinary type . . . with a critical Introduction, Annotations, and Facsimiles," was issued by Scrivener in 1864 (*Bezæ Codex Cantabrigiensis*, etc.), and a collation of the readings of the Codex by Eb. Nestle (*Novi Testamenti Græci Supplementum*, 1896). To these two the student is referred until the appearance of the new photogravure reproduction, now preparing under the direction of the Cambridge authorities. *Scrivener's edition and Nestle's collation.*

A restoration of the "Western" or Roman text of Acts and Luke has been attempted by Fried. Blass in his *Acta Apostolorum*, 1896 (ed. Minor), and his *Evangelium secundum Lucam*, 1897. Compare, also, his *Editio Philologica* of Acts, 1895.[2] *Blass's restoration of the "Western" text of Acts and Luke's Gospel.*

The present extraordinary interest in Codex Bezæ is due, not so much to the fact of its variations from some given text, the Receptus or Westcott and Hort,

[1] William Whiston, *Primitive New Testament*, 1747. He also translated the Codex Claromontanus (Paul) and the Codex Alexandrinus (Catholic Epistles). Thomas Kipling, *Codex Theodori Bezæ Cantabrigiensis*, 1793.

[2] See O. von Gebhardt, article "Bibeltext," Herzog's *Real-Encyklopädie*, Bd. II, S. 743. C. A. Briggs, *Study of Holy Scripture*, 1899, 200 ff. H. Trabaud, "Un Curieux Manuscrit du Nouveau Testament," *Revue de Théol. et de Phil.*, 1896, 378 ff. Gregory's Prolegomena, or any good Introduction, as Holtzmann, Jülicher, Weiss, Salmon.

for instance, as to the uniqueness of its variations. In addition to the ordinary inaccuracies due to the writer of the Codex, or his archetype, or both, and the usual corruptions common to all codices, Codex D exhibits certain characteristic tendencies; such as the love for adding or recasting words, clauses, or sentences, and for harmonising apparently contradictory passages. As a specimen of the additions which this Codex alone contributes, see Luke 6. After the fourth verse we read, "On the same day, as He (Jesus) beheld a man labouring on the Sabbath, he said to him: Man, if thou knowest what thou doest, blessed art thou; if however thou dost not know, cursed art thou and a transgressor of the law." In Luke 11 : 2, between the words "pray" and "say," we read, "Use not vain repetitions as the rest do, for some think that they shall be heard for their much speaking. On the contrary, when ye pray," etc. In Acts 12 : 10, after "they went out," there is added, "and they descended the seven steps." In Acts 10 : 25, we find, "When Peter drew near unto Cæsarea, one of the slaves ran forward and announced his arrival. And Cornelius jumped up." In Acts 11 : 27, after "Antioch," there is added, "and there was great rejoicing. And we being assembled," etc. This addition is interesting in the light of the so-called we-sections in Acts.

It must not, however, be assumed from these few examples, that all the contributions of this Codex are alike interesting and valuable. As a matter of fact,

the tendency of Codex Bezæ is to "conflate" the text, and thus most of the contributions are nothing more than simple glosses.[1] Furthermore, it must not be assumed that D stands alone in its variations. Rather it is a member of an ancient and honourable family.

[1] For detailed proof, see B. Weiss, *Der Codex D in der Apostelgeschichte* (*Texte und Untersuchungen*, XVII, 1897).

The form of text which it preserves is supported by many Church Fathers of the second and following centuries, and by the Old Latin and Syriac Versions. Thus, although the Codex itself dates from the beginning of the sixth century, yet the type of text which it represents is traceable as far back as the second century. It is to be found, for instance, in Cyprian and Tertullian at Carthage, and in Irenæus at Lyons, where Codex Bezæ was discovered; and traces of it appear in Clement and Origen at Alexandria, as well as at Rome.[1]

(marginal note: Type of text traceable to second century.)

The Old Latin Versions, and the Versions in Syriac (Curetonian, Philoxenian, Lewis), likewise present a similar type of text. In fact, it is generally admitted that about the year 200 a type of text similar to that of Codex Bezæ was spread abroad in Syria and in the West. Nay, more, traces of this text may possibly exist in Justin Martyr and Marcion, that is, as early as the first half of the second century, and thus it may be that Codex D represents the oldest edition of the New Testament books which gained a wide circulation.[2] To this type of text the term " Western " has been applied since the time of Semler, and has been appropriated also by Hort.[3] It is a conventional symbol, and has no distinctively geographical signification. It is to the East that most scholars look for the origin of the Western text, and specifically to Syria and Antioch. Thence it spread over the lines of commerce to Southern Gaul, Carthage, Rome, and Alexandria. Codex Bezæ thus does not stand alone. The majority of its typical characteristics are to be found

(marginal note: The term " Western " has no geographical signification.)

---

[1] See P. Corssen, *Der Cyprianische Text der Acta Apostolorum*, Berlin, 1892. Hort, Introduction, 113.

[2] See W. Bousset, *Theologische Rundschau*, I, 406–416, Juli, 1898, S. 410.

[3] See Gregory's Prolegomena, 188. Hort, Introduction. 113.

M

throughout the entire Western group. Thus, in Matt.
20 : 28, we find D supported in its insertion, or in
Luke 10 : 42; 22 : 19–20; 23 : 34, supported in its
omissions. Bearing in mind, therefore, that Codex
Bezæ is a member of a family, and the Baconian
warning as to the vice of neglecting negative instances, we proceed to give a summary of recent
opinions concerning the type of text represented by
this Codex.

1. Theory of Latinisation held by Mill, Wetstein, J. R. Harris.

1. *Theory of Latinisation.* — In facing a Græco-Latin
codex the first question is : Is the Greek text de-
pendent upon the Latin, or is each independent ? The
prevailing view up to the time of Griesbach was that
the Western Greek text is due to a readjustment to
the Latin Versions (so Mill, Wetstein). This "whim-
sical" (Hort) theory, given up by Griesbach and his
successors, is defended by J. Rendel Harris (*Study of
the Codex Bezæ,* 1891), who attempts to prove " that
the whole of the Greek text of Codex Bezæ, from the
beginning of Matthew to the end of Acts, is a readjustment of an earlier text to the Latin Version."
"The Greek has no certain value except where it
differs from its own Latin, and must not any longer be
regarded as an independent authority." And three
years later (*Four Lectures on the Western Text,* 1894,
73), " The Bezan Latin is more archaic than the Bezan
Greek."

2. Chase's theory of Syriacisa- tion.

2. *Theory of Syriacisation.* — Professor Harris's
study induced another Cambridge scholar, Professor
F. H. Chase, to investigate the Codex, and especially
the text of Acts, with the result that " the Bezan Greek
is moulded on a Syrian text," a conclusion which
seemed to disprove the theory of Latinisation.[1] In
his study, Professor Chase was led to assume the

---

[1] F. H. Chase, *The Old Syriac Element in Codex Bezæ,* 1893.

existence of an old Syriac text of the Acts, of which Hort had said, twelve years previously, "Nothing as yet is known" (Introduction, 85). Professor Harris, in a review of Professor Chase's book, thinks he has removed the hypothesis of an old Syriac text of Acts into the region of fact (an opinion which seems to have been confirmed by the discovery of Mrs. Lewis), but does not feel himself compelled to give up the theory of Latinisation.[1]

Probably no one theory explains all the variations in the text of the Codex. The Latinisation theory may explain some, the Syriacisation theory others; while the usual theory that the Latin has been adjusted to the Greek may explain still others. It cannot be said that the Codex represents the only pure text, as Bornemann,[2] nor that it is the most depraved text, as Burgon.[3] At all events, the relation of Codex Bezæ to the Old Latin and Old Syriac texts seems to have been established. *{No one theory explains all the variations.}*

3. *Theory of Jewish-Christian Origin.* — Dr. Resch is in search of an original Gospel in Hebrew. He is interested in every possible genuine "agraphon," any Hebraising text which may point to an original Hebrew text, and any variants in the Gospel texts or in the citations of the Fathers. The variants, therefore, in the Gospels of Codex Bezae and its Western relatives are of immense importance to him. He holds with Credner the theory of the Jewish-Christian origin of the Codex Bezae, though, unlike Credner, he recognises its relation to the Old Latin and Old Syriac texts, and, like Professor Harris, holds that a primitive bilingual existed before the time of Tatian. The "un- *{3. Resch's and Credner's theory of Jewish-Christian origin.}*

---

[1] See Hackmann on Chase, *Theol. Litz.*, 1894; col. 604–609. Harris, *Four Lectures*, etc., 14 ff.

[2] *Acta Apostolorum*, etc., I, 1848.

[3] *Revision Revised*, 12.

known authority " of Credner, which lies at the back of the Western text as one of its sources, is identified by Resch with a secondary translation of the original Hebrew Gospel. The "great unknown" of Credner, Professor Bousset thinks, has a good deal of the ghost in it. Dr. Resch's theory has met with little acceptance among scholars. Professor Harris does not think the theory impossible, but notes that the palæographical facts are against it. Professor Ropes, in his review of Resch's *Agrapha,* feels certain that the theory of Jewish-Christian origin has been conclusively refuted.[1]

4. Blass's theory of two editions of Acts and Luke.

4. *Theory of Two Editions of Acts and Luke.* — To be considered more at length is the theory of the philologist, Professor Friedrich Blass of Halle, first published in an article entitled *Twofold Tradition of the Text in Acts* (1894), and in its latest form extended now to the Gospel of Luke (1897). The reader is referred especially to the Præfatio in his *Evangelium secundum Lucam* (1897), although there is some additional material in his *Philology of the Gospels* (1898). Professor Blass has written extensively in support of his theory, confining his attention at first to the double form of the text in Acts. His theory, as first stated, is that Luke issued two copies, a rough draft, represented by the Western text, and the corrected and less prolix copy, represented by the usual text. The former

---

[1] See A. Resch, *Aussercanonische Paralleltexte zu den Evangelien,* 1893–96 (*Texte und Untersuchungen,* X, 1–4). K. A. Credner, *Beiträge zur Einleitung in die biblischen Schriften,* 1832, I, 452–518. J. R. Harris, *Four Lectures,* etc., 4; 1-13. W. Bousset, *Die Evangeliencitate Justins des Märtyrers,* 1891, S. 7. Paul Ewald, *Das Hauptproblem der Evangelienfrage u. s. w.,* 1890, holds to Credner's theory. J. H. Ropes, *Die Sprüche Jesu,* 1896, a careful sifting of Resch's *Agrapha.* Also review by him and Professor Torrey in *American Journal of Theology,* April, 1899.

was designed for Roman readers, the latter for Theophilus.[1]

The theory of two editions is not new. Joannes Clericus, in the last century, was almost of the opinion that Luke edited the Acts twice (*Acta Apostolorum,* ed. Minor, III. Reference to Clericus or Hemsterhuis not exact). Hort also had thought that "the purely documentary phenomena (were) compatible with the supposition that the Western and the non-Western texts started respectively from a first and a second edition of the Gospels, both conceivably apostolic" (Introduction, 177), but dismisses the theory on internal grounds. Lightfoot also had suggested that "the Evangelist himself might have issued two separate editions" of his Gospel and also of the Acts.[2] Professor Zahn also, in the winter of 1885–86, had come to the opinion that the Bezan text of Acts represents "either the rough draft of the author before publication, or the copy

The two-edition theory not new. Clericus, Zahn, Lightfoot.

---

[1] The *Philology of the Gospels* is a dilution of his admirable preface to Luke, adapted to English readers who do not read Latin. Professor C. R. Gregory, in a review of the book (*American Journal of Theology*, October, 1898, 881), calls it a series of "rambling observations." The title " Philology " is certainly misleading, as is that of " Gospels."

For convenience, the following list of Professor Blass's writings on the subject is appended : —

Stud. u. Krit. 1894, S. 86–120, " Die Zweifache Textüberlieferung in der Apostelgeschichte." *Neue kirchliche Zeitschr.* 1895, S. 712–725, "Ueber die verschiedenen Textesformen in den Schriften des Lucas." *Hermathena,* 1895, 121–143 (IX, No. 31), "De duplici forma Actorum Lucæ." *Acta Apostolorum,* Editio Philologica, 1895. *Stud. u. Krit.* 1896, S. 436–471, " Neue Texteszeugen für die Apostelgeschichte." *Ibid.,* S. 733 ff. (on Luke 22 : 15 ff.). *Acta Apostolorum* (ed. Minor), 1896. *Hermathena,* 1896, 291 ff., " De Variis Formis Evangelii Lucani." *Evangelium secundum Lucam,* 1897. *Philology of the Gospels,* 1898.

[2] *Fresh Revision of the English New Testament,* 1873, 43.

(Handexemplar) belonging to the author, along with supplementary marginal notes."[1]   But Blass deserves whatever credit there is in the theory.   At first, as has been noted, Blass spoke of "rough draft" and "corrected copy."   The Western text corresponded with the former, and the usual text with the latter.   When, however, he applied the hypothesis to the Gospel of Luke, he found that the Western text of Luke corresponded with the corrected copy, while the usual text corresponded with the rough draft; or, in a word, that the text-phenomena in Acts and in Luke were dissimilar (*Evang. Luc.*, V ff. *Acta*, ed. Minor, V., *Philology*, etc., 103).   An amendment to the theory became necessary.   The theory as amended "requires merely one older copy and one more recent."[2]   The more recent copy is abridged, the work "becoming somewhat tedious for the author, or at least losing something of its freshness for him, so that he was naturally disposed to omit many unessential circumstances and details which he formerly had given."[3]   The curious result is that the abridged edition of the Gospel is represented by the Western text, that of Acts by the non-Western text.   Theophilus gets an unabridged edition of the Gospel, and an abridged edition of Acts; while the readers in Rome get an abridged edition of the Gospel and an unabridged edition of Acts.   Both seem to have been content with the arrangement.   In support of the theory for Acts, Blass urges (1) that the language of the additions and variants of the Western text is Lucan, and (2) that the additions themselves are possible only to a contemporary, that is, to the author himself.[4]   At this point Blass remarks that it is easier to test the insertions of the Western (or as he

Blass forced to amend his original theory.

---

[1] *Einleitung in das Neue Testament*, Bd. II, 1899, S. 338–359.   Compare S. 348.

[2] *Philology*, 126.   [3] *Ibid.*, 104.   [4] *Ibid.*, 113 ff., 119 ff.

prefers to call it, Roman) text of Acts than to test the omissions of the Western text of the Gospel, and, hence, that it is easier to defend the theory of two editions in the case of Acts than in the case of Luke.[1] In applying his theory to the Gospel, he notes the difficulty of restoring the Western text. Conflations and assimilations are more prevalent in the Synoptic Gospels than elsewhere, and so therefore in Luke. The pure Western text of the Latin palimpsest of Fleury and the Greek Codex Laudianus are unavailable for Luke. Justin Martyr cannot be used. The texts, therefore, upon which he must rely — the Old Latin and Syriac Versions, Tatian, Marcion, the Ferrar-Group — represent a mixed type of text, that is, give us a mixture of the Western or Roman and the non-Western or Antiochian. Thus we are left largely to the Greek of Codex Bezæ for a relatively unmixed Western text. In Acts, the characteristic of the Bezan text is its additions; in Luke, however, it is its omissions.[2]

Theory of two editions more easily defended in Acts than in Luke's Gospel.

In Luke's Gospel, then, Blass begins with the omissions, and selects as test cases 8 : 43; 10 : 41; 12 : 19; 19 : 29; and concludes that the abridgments cannot be explained away as spurious, and that, therefore, as genuine, they are evidence of two editions. Coming next to the relatively few cases of insertion, he treats first the story of the man working on the Sabbath (6 : 5), and notes that it has a genuine ring, although indeed no Church Father records this tradition.[3] The reason that Luke omitted the story in his edition for Theophilus was, that it might give offence to Christian Jews, while the Roman readers would find in the nar-

---

[1] *Philology*, 103, 141.

[2] On the Ferrar-Group, see J. Rendel Harris, *On the Origin of the Ferrar-Group*, 1893.

[3] See Ropes, *Die Sprüche Jesu*, S. 124-126.

rative no occasion of stumbling.[1] Similarly, the Ferrar-Group attributes the section about the woman
taken in adultery (John 7 : 53–8 : 11) to Luke, inserting it after Luke 21 : 38. Blass, however, thinks the
section should be put two verses earlier, and after
some further conjectures notes that the language of
the section is Lucan. The reason that Luke omitted
in his copy for Theophilus, and inserted in the copy
for Rome, is precisely the same as in the former case.
It is evident, however, that Blass is not so confident
either of his restoration of the text, or of his theory
of two editions in the case of the Gospel, as he is in the
case of Acts. He admits that the text phenomena in
Luke are not easily solvable, and says he is "very far
from pretending this solution to be, as it were, a key
which unlocks all doors."[2]

The theory attracted the attention of scholars immediately, and has found favour in the eyes of several
critics, as Nestle, Belser, and Salmon. This consent
may be due, as Bousset suggests, to apologetic inter-
ests. Zöckler and Zahn were inclined to approve it for
Acts, though not for the Gospel. On the other hand,
the theory was contested by other scholars. Corssen,
for instance, has attempted to show the un-Lucan
character of the Roman text, and Ramsay thinks the
text has "a fatal smoothness: it loses the rather harsh
but very individual style of Luke, and it neglects some
of the literary forms that Luke observed." It gives
a mixed but valuable second-century text, shows a
second-century interpretation of various passages, and
adds several good bits of information, though they
were not written by Luke, except perhaps in a few
cases (*Expositor*, 1897, 469).[3]

John 7 : 53–8 : 11 attributed to Luke.

Reception of Blass's theory.

---

[1] *Evang. Luc.*, XLVI–XLVII.   [2] *Philology*, 168.

[3] See Blass, *Præfatio in Lucam*, where he meets some of the
objections. E. Nestle, *Einführung in das Griechische Neue*

5. *Theory of Bernhard Weiss.*—There is no sturdier opponent of the theory of Blass than Professor Weiss of Berlin. In his study of the Bezan text he does not propose to examine the hypothesis of two editions as such, but rather to determine whether the Western text of Acts is earlier or later than that of the ancient majuscules. His theory is that the Western text has almost no authority whatever. In emphasising, therefore, the almost complete worthlessness of the Western text, he tacitly endeavours to shatter the hypothesis of Blass. Looking carefully at all negative instances, and weighing the evidence of the majority of the variants, Weiss obtains antecedent probability against the genuineness of the Western readings. The usual corruptions in D are no more peculiar to D than to other codices. Moreover, there is a motive discernible in the recasting of the text, namely, to change purposely the older majuscules. Now of two texts, the one which is more easily explained from the other is secondary. Thus B, far from having variants which are Lucan, is rather a "reflektierte Nachbesserung" of the older majuscules. The Western and non-

Testament," S. 100, 101. J. Belser (R. C.), *Beiträge zur Erklärung der Apostelgeschichte*, 1897. G. Salmon, *Introduction to the New Testament*, 1897, 592 ff. Ibid., *Some Thoughts on the Textual Criticism of the New Testament*, 1897. W. Bousset, *Theologische Rundschau*, 1898, I, 413. O. Zöckler, *Studia Gryphiswaldensia*, 1895, S. 132 ff. The. Zahn, *Einleitung in das Neue Testament*, 1899, II, S. 338 ff., 346. O. Zöckler, *Beweis des Glaubens*, 1898, S. 28–35. Corssen, *Gött. gel. Anz.* 1896, S. 425 ff. W. M. Ramsay, *St. Paul the Traveller and the Roman Citizen*, 3d ed., 1897, 25. Ibid., *The Church in the Roman Empire*, 3d ed., 1894, 151–165. Also *Expositor*, 1895, 129 ff., 212 ff. ; 1897, 460–471.

Against Blass see also Jülicher, *Einleitung in das Neue Testament*, 1894, S. 271. H. Holtzmann, *Th. Litz.*, 1896, No. 3 ; 1898, col. 535–539. W. Bousset, *Theologische Rundschau*, 1898, I, 406–416.

The Western and non-Western texts not independent witnesses.

Western texts are not independent witnesses: the former depends upon the latter. The changes, to be sure, are early, arising long before the canonisation of Acts. They do not appear, with slight exceptions, in the speeches of Acts. "Nowhere in the matter of the text is anything essentially changed, or a new point added in reference to the movements of the history." The changes themselves are not uniform in character. Some are unique, most are akin to the changes common to all texts. The Western readings therefore have no independent authority whatever, and can certainly not be attributed to one hand as the Blass theory requires.[1]

Summary of objections to Blass's theory.

The objections to the theory of Blass may be summed up as follows: (1) Its simplicity is really an argument against it. Phenomena so complex demand a more complex solvent than is furnished by a single hypothesis. (2) The uniform character of the variants demanded by the hypothesis is made *à priori* unlikely by the striking dissimilarity of the Western text of Acts from that of Luke. Moreover, Blass has not proved the uniform character of the variants. (3) The motive assigned for the omission in the copy for Theophilus and the insertion in the copy for Roman readers of such sections as that of the man working on the Sabbath, or of the woman taken in adultery, — the motive, namely, that the Jewish Christians would be offended, — cannot be taken seriously. Why are not other uncomfortable words of Jesus about the law omitted in the copy for Theophilus? (4) The motive likewise for abridging one copy each of the Gospel and of Acts, namely, that the author found his work tedious, cannot be considered a serious argument. (5)

[1] See B. Weiss, "Der Codex D in der Apostelgeschichte, 1897, *Texte und Untersuchungen*, XVII. Compare "Die Apostelgeschichte," 1893, *Texte und Untersuchungen*, IX, 3, 4.

The text-phenomena of Luke do not require the two-edition hypothesis, any more than those of Mark or Matthew or John. Starting with the variants of Luke, and then passing over to Acts, even these unique readings in Acts may be explained on other grounds more successfully. (6) The great fault is the neglect of negative instances. Instead of starting with a few brilliant readings, he should have begun with the great majority of ordinary readings. The analogy of the phenomena of the Western text as a whole should have been the basis of the opinion on a few brilliant readings in the Bezan text of Acts. Blass should have given a careful and systematic study to the Western texts as a whole, before asserting his theory on the basis chiefly of one codex.

6. *Theory of Westcott and Hort.* — Westcott and Hort think that Tischendorf, under the influence of the Sinaiticus, and without definite principles, has admitted too many Western readings into his editions. They feel that these readings, when confronted with their rivals, generate a sense of distrust, which distrust is but increased upon further and intimate acquaintance. To be sure, Codex Bezæ, more clearly than any other extant Greek manuscript, reveals a type of text most widely read in the third, and probably in the second century; but, they bid us notice, antiquity and purity are not synonymous terms. The tendency of the Western texts is toward fulness, conflation, in which tendency they stand unrivalled. The motive in all this is apparent. It is hard, however, to explain omissions in a type of text whose characteristic is fulness. In comparing the non-Western texts with the Western texts at the points where the latter omit and the former retain, we are led to the hypothesis that what are omissions in these Western texts are interpolations in the usually trustworthy non-Western

texts. Thus only one class of phenomena in the Western readings can claim attention, namely, the omissions, or, more correctly, the non-interpolations. The theory of Westcott and Hort is the theory of Western non-interpolations. They therefore stand midway between Weiss and Blass in their estimate of the Western type of text. But have they given sufficient prominence to Western readings? On their principle, a small handful of Western authorities may, at times, overthrow the combined authority of B and ℵ, while, at other times, B holds the field alone against the combined armies of West and East. This difficulty has led to the warning against a "Westcott and Hort ab omnibus receptus."

Westcott and Hort midway between Blass and Weiss in estimate of the Western text.

7. *Theory of Professor Salmon.* — The Dublin scholar thinks that Westcott and Hort have given us the text as read in Alexandria, probably in the third century, and possibly before the end of the second. But there existed at the same time in Rome a text which differed in some respects from the Alexandrian text. The trouble with Dr. Hort is that he does not admit the possibility of an independent Western tradition.[1] It would seem as if he were under the influence of a preconceived theory as to the existence of original autographs. But suppose there are editors at work in the Synoptic Gospels. Can we speak of the individual writings of the individual authors in the light of the traces of the secondary character, say of the First Gospel?[2] The textual critic must take into account the Synoptic Problem. And further, suppose, with Blass, that there are two editions of the Third Gospel and the Acts. Which is the original autograph? "If we desire a text absolutely free from ambiguity, we desire what God has never been pleased to give His church."[3]

Professor Salmon. A text at Rome differing from the Alexandrian.

---

[1] *Some Thoughts*, etc., 56.   [2] *Ibid.*, etc., 105.

[3] *Ibid.*, etc., 130.

Coming now to the theory of Blass, Dr. Salmon points out the fact that the documentary evidence is too late to give us " authentic information as to the circumstances of their first publication." [1] There is, therefore, no " external evidence enabling us either to confirm or to reject the hypothesis of a double edition." Internal evidence must decide. [2] Now, although the reconstruction of the Western text given by Blass does not commend itself *in toto* to Salmon, there are, nevertheless, some variations which rest upon the authority of Luke. [3] Blass has made out a good case for Acts, [4] and probably a similar hypothesis would cover the facts in the Gospel. But the dissimilarity of the text-phenomena in the Gospel and in Acts, and the inherent difficulties in the text of the Gospels, arising from early conformations, make an alternative theory to that of Blass more probable for the Gospel, namely, that explanatory readings were given by Luke in Rome and were preserved in the West. There was, however, no definite written text; otherwise we could reproduce it now. Rather the explanatory readings are added to the Alexandrian text as of coördinate and equal authority, since there was no theory of verbal inspiration to molest or to make afraid. [5] Thus the Roman text differs from the Alexandrian as a second edition of a book differs from the first. [6] At all events, the Western variations are not the licentious additions of audacious scribes, but many of them represent the form in which the Gospel was read in the church of Rome in apostolic or subapostolic times. [7]

The objective summary of recent opinion upon Codex

Hypothesis of a double edition to be decided by internal evidence only.

---

[1] *Some Thoughts*, etc., 134.
[2] Compare Hort, Introduction, 177.
[3] *Some Thoughts*, etc., 137.
[4] *Ibid.*, etc., 139.
[5] *Ibid.*, etc., 147-151.
[6] *Ibid.*, etc., 158.
[7] *Ibid.*, etc., 151.　　See also G. Salmon's *Introduction to the New Testament*, 8th ed., 1897, 592 ff.

Professor
Harris on
the Bezan
text.
Bezæ and its relatives attempted above will, I think, enable the reader to appreciate the suggestive remark of Professor Harris, with which I conclude the sketch. " The more we think of it, the more complex does the Bezan text become. It has passed through the hands of a number of people of active mind, whose remarks are stratified in the Western text: they are not all of them Syrians, and it is not yet even proved that there are no Western expansions which are original. The whole history of the text requires renewed and careful inquisition, without prejudice in favour of the solvent power of a single hypothesis." [1]

Review of
the history
of Textual
Criticism of
the New
Testament.
In reviewing the history of Textual Criticism of the New Testament we have marked, in the beginning, the superstitious reverence for the text which opposed all attempts to investigate or amend it; but, with a strange inconsistency, attached itself, not to the Greek Original, but to its Latin representative. We have marked the transference of the same superstition to a Greek text based upon a few late and inferior manuscripts, and invested with a factitious authority through the audacity of a clever publisher. We have marked the slow process of unseating this textual idol, the resolute assertion by scholars of the authority of the most ancient witnesses, and the efforts to bring the New Testament text into accordance with their testimony. We have marked the formulation of textual principles and the development of critical methods.

A real
advance.
There has been a great and real advance. It has come to be accepted that Scripture is not a fetich, but is fairly open, like other literary productions, to the same critical tests which are applied to other literature, and that such criticism, so far from implying irreverence, is one of the highest marks of respect that can be shown toward the Bible.

[1] *Four Lectures*, etc., 89.

The Textus Receptus has been remanded to its proper place as a historical monument, and has been summarily rejected as a basis for a correct text.

In weighing the evidence for readings, the emphasis has been shifted from the number to the quality of manuscripts. In other words, it is an accepted principle that manuscripts are to be weighed and not counted.

It is recognised that every class of textual facts is to be taken into account; that internal evidence is to be subordinated to external evidence, and that conclusions as to the character and relative importance of manuscripts are to be reached by a study of their affinities; in other words, by the application of the genealogical method.

Still, much remains to be done. "Whoever should conclude," says Dr. Nestle, "that New Testament criticism has reached its goal, would greatly err. As the archæologist in Olympia or Delphi exhumes the shattered temples, and essays to recombine the fragments in their ancient splendour, so, much labour is still needed before all the stones shall have been collected, and the sanctuary of the New Testament writings restored to its original form." *Much still to be done.*

The noble work of Westcott and Hort, by its wide range, its laborious research and its boldness, has commanded a large measure of assent, but it cannot be said to be decisive, even as the consensus respecting it is by no means universal. There is some danger of Westcott and Hort's text coming to be regarded as a second Textus Receptus. It has taken time to grasp their principles and method. Professor Salmon justly remarks that "the foundations of their system are buried out of sight of ordinary readers of their work. Their theories are based on immense inductions, in the course of which they must, with enormous labour, have tabulated comparative lists of the peculiarities of *The work of Westcott and Hort not final.*

manuscripts or groups of manuscripts." Eighteen years, however, have enabled critics to digest, and to apprehend their processes and conclusions as a whole, with the result of calling forth more than one ringing challenge. Their theory of the double recension of the text in the middle of the third century, their genealogical nomenclature, and their too exclusive reliance upon the testimony of B and ℵ are alike the subjects of incisive criticism.

Results from studies of D not final. The results evolved from the special studies of Codex Bezæ are alike suggestive and promising, but cannot be accepted as final.

With gratitude for the substantial gains, both in material and in method, since the appearance of Erasmus's first edition, we must still be content to wait.

Activity of special scholarship and archæological research. Meanwhile, accurate special scholarship is busy in testing the old positions, exposing weak points, or detecting fresh confirmations. Archæological research is diligent, and such discoveries as the Gospel of Peter, the Lewis palimpsest, and the Oxyrhynchus fragments afford promises and prophecies of other discoveries which may lead the student nearer to the primitive sources of New Testament Scripture, and settle many questions which are still in dispute.

Toward one result the course of textual criticism appears to be slowly but surely moving — the modification and, in part, the abandonment of the idea of original autographs as an object of search. Whether the theory of the double editions of Acts and Luke be vindicated or not, whatever may be the final decision concerning the documents represented in Acts, enough has been developed to make it evident that different forms of a New Testament document may be due to the author himself, and that editorship may have enlarged, modified, or changed the form in which the document originally came from the author's pen.

APPENDIX

The following list is added of books of reference not elsewhere mentioned.

PALÆOGRAPHY

V. Gardthausen: *Griechische Palaeographie*. Leipzig, 1879.

Fried. Blass: *Palaeographie, Bücherwesen und Handschriften-kunde*. In Müller, *Handbuch der klass. Alterthumswissenschaft*. 2 Ausg. Bd. I. München, 1892.

W. Wattenbach: *Anleitung zur griech. Palaeographie*. 2 Ausg. Leipzig, 1877.

Ibid.: *Scripturæ Græcæ Specimina*. Berlin, 1883.

Ibid. and A. von Velsen: *Exempla Codicum Græcorum litt. minusc. scriptorum*. Heidelberg, 1878. Fol. 50 plates.

Ibid.: *Schrifttafeln zur Geschichte der Griechischen Schrift*. 1877.

E. A. Bond and E. M. Thompson: *Facsimiles of Ancient Manuscripts*. Palæographical Society of London, 1873–82.

T. W. Allen: *Notes on Abbreviations in Greek Manuscripts*. With facsimiles. Oxford, 1889.

W. A. Copinger: *The Bible and its Transmission*. With 28 facsimiles. London, 1897.

AUTOGRAPHS

J. R. Harris: *New Testament Autographs*. Supplement to American Journal of Philology, No. 12. Baltimore, 1882.

CRITICAL EDITIONS OF THE GREEK TESTAMENT

C. Tischendorf: *Novum Testamentum Græce*. Editio Octava Critica Major. 3 vols. Prolegomena, III, by C. R. Gregory. Leipzig, 1869–94.

A small edition of the text of the 8th ed. with a selection of readings, 1878.

Ed. by O. von Gebhardt, with variants of Tregelles and Westcott and Hort. 5th ed. 1891.

B. F. Westcott and F. J. A. Hort: *The New Testament in the Original Greek.* 2 vols. American edition, with an Introduction by Philip Schaff. New York. 3d ed. 1883.

E. Palmer: *The Greek Testament with the Readings adopted by the Revisers of the Authorised Version, and with References in the Margin to Parallel Passages of the Old and New Testament.* Oxford, Clarendon Press, 1882. Very handsome typography. An edition in smaller type, with a wide margin for notes.

F. H. A. Scrivener: *Novum Testamentum. Textus Stephanici.* With various readings of Beza, the Elzevirs, Lachmann, Tischendorf, Tregelles, Westcott and Hort, and the revisers. Cambridge and London, 1887. New readings at the foot of the page, and the displaced readings of the text in heavier type.

W. Sanday: Lloyd's edition of Mill's text, with parallel references, Eusebian Canons, etc., and three Appendices (published separately), containing variants of Westcott and Hort, and a selection of important readings with authorities, together with readings from Oriental Versions, Memphitic, Armenian, and Ethiopic. Oxford, 1889.

R. F. Weymouth: *The Resultant Greek Testament.* Readings of Stephen (1550), Lachmann, Tregelles, Lightfoot, and (for the Pauline Epistles) Ellicott. Also of Alford and Weiss for Matthew, the Basle edition, Westcott and Hort, and the revisers. London, 1892.

J. Baljon: *Novum Testamentum Græce præsertim in usum studiosorum.* Groningæ, 1898. W. Bousset (Theologische Rundschau, July, 1898, S. 416) characterises it as often a bad, inaccurate, unsystematic excerpt from Tischendorf's 8thMaj. The readings of Persian, Ethiopic, and Armenian Versions are untrustworthy, even in Tischendorf.

E. Nestle: *Testamentum Novum Græce cum Apparatu Critico.* Stuttgart, 1898. Will not save the use of editions with the manuscript variants.

F. Schjott: *Novum Testamentum Græce ad fidem Testium Vetustissimorum cognovit.* Adds various readings from the Elzevirs and Tischendorf.

Fried. Blass: *Acta Apostolorum sive Lucæ ad Theophilum Liber Alter secundum formam quæ videtur Romanam.* Leipzig, 1896.

Ibid.: *Evangelium secundum Lucam sive Lucæ ad Theophilum Liber Prior secundum Formam quæ videtur Romanam.* Leipzig, 1897.

CONVENIENT MANUALS

Eb. Nestle: *Einführung in das griechische Neue Testament.* Göttingen, 1897.

C. E. Hammond: *Outlines of Textual Criticism applied to the New Testament.* 5th rev. ed. Oxford, 1890.

F. G. Kenyon: *Our Bible and the Ancient Manuscripts.* 3d ed. London, 1897.

P. Schaff: *A Companion to the Greek Testament and the English Version.* 3d rev. ed. New York, 1888.

B. B. Warfield: *An Introduction to the Textual Criticism of the New Testament.* New York, 1887.

E. C. Mitchell: *The Critical Handbook of the Greek New Testament.* New edition. New York, 1896. Useful catalogue of manuscripts.

A catalogue of editions of the Greek Testament, prepared by the late Dr. Isaac H. Hall, may be found in Schaff's *Companion.*

INDEX

Abbot, Ezra, 12, 57, 120, 123, 129, 143
Accents, 8, 19
Achelis, H., 41
Adler, J. G. C., 98
Alcalà, 49, 50
Aldus Manutius, 48, 53
Alford, H., 138
Alter, F. K., 98
Ambrose, 40
Ammonian sections, 9, 10, 21, 22
Ammonius, 9, 10
Apostolic Fathers, 38
Aristion, 35
Athos, Mt., 97, 136
Augusti, 104
Autographs, 2, 3, 4, 77, 176

Baethgen, 33
Barberini readings, 67
Barnabas, Epistle of, 16, 17
Bartolocci, 130
Bebb, L. J. M., 41
Belser, J., 168, 169
Bengel, J. A., 76, 87–89, 90
Bensley, R. L., 31, 33
Bentley, Richard, 69, 70, 139
  Proposals of, 70–75
Berger, S., 28
Berlin Academy, 37
Bertheau, C., 93, 129
Beza, Theo., 58, 63, 158
Birch, A., 98, 130
Blass, F., 159, 164–168
Bloomfield, S. T., 115
Bodleian Library, 23, 34
Bonwetsch, G., 41
Bosworth and Waring, 35

Bousset, W., 164, 169
Breathings, 8, 19
Briggs, C. A., 159
British Museum, 14, 19, 28, 34
British and Foreign Bible Society, 23
Burgon, J. W., 41, 61, 119–121, 137, 141, 142, 152, 158
Burk, P. D., 89, 90
Burkitt, F. C., 27, 31, 33

Cambridge University Library, 22
Canons of Criticism
  Bengel, 88
  Griesbach, 102
  Lachmann, 112
  Scrivener, 141
  Tischendorf, 125–129
  Tregelles, 132–134
Capitals in manuscripts, 20
Chapters, division into, 12
Chase, F. H., 162
Christian VII., 98
Chrysostom, 148, 149
Clement of Rome, Epistle of, 20, 38
Clement of Alexandria, 37, 41, 148, 161
Clericus, J., 165.
Codices
  Alexandrinus, 11, 19, 64
  Amiatinus, 114, 131, 135
  Basilianus, 14, 135
  Bezæ, 14, 22, 62, 157–174, 176
  Boernerianus, 99
  Borgianus, 23
  Claromontanus, 14, 22